The Wonderful Madness of Becoming

A HORSE OF
A DIFFERENT COLOR

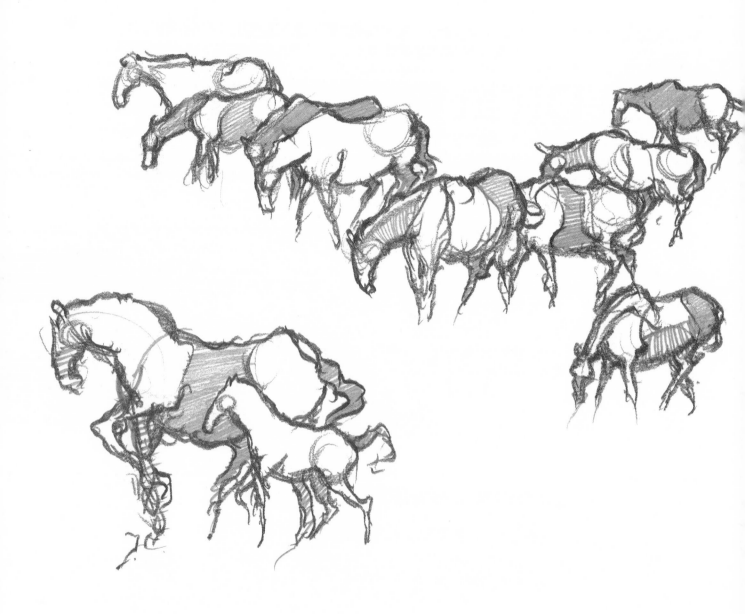

The Wonderful Madness of Becoming

A HORSE OF
A DIFFERENT COLOR

Letters, Drawings & Quotes
Presented by

WILLIAM ARTHUR
HERRING

President, Knickerbocker Artists • USA

RED TREE PUBLISHING CO.

CLINT, TEXAS

FIRST EDITION

ISBN 0-9639145-0-2
Library of Congress Catalog Card Number 93-086671

Cover art: "Santa Fe Horses," pastel, by William A. Herring PSA:
permanent collection of Dr. Daria Muzychka, MD.

"You have everything
but one thing, madness.
A man needs a little
madness
or else—

he
never
dares
cut
the
rope
and
be
free."

—Zorba the Greek

GALLERIES REPRESENTING THE ARTIST:

Joan Cawley Galleries
Santa Fe, New Mexico
Scottsdale, Arizona

E. S. Lawrence Gallery
Taos, New Mexico

Palmer's Gallery 800
Hot Springs National Park, Arkansas

Perry House Galleries
Old Towne Alexandria, Virginia

Wilder Expressions
Longview, Texas

Studio W
El Paso, Texas

Jan Herring Summer Gallery
Cloudcroft, New Mexico

CONTENTS

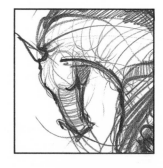

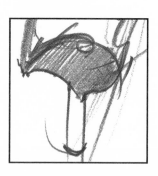

INTRODUCTION

I was thirty-five and not quite sure about becoming a professional artist. Raised by one, and often in the company of artists, I found them the kind that often made my blood boil. It must be confessed, however, that I had just finished a ten year journey through the lives of the "great dead ones, the masters," and I was already put off by their disgusting record at becoming commendable human beings. I was biased.

For ten years I had been training under the mentorship of my mother, Jan Herring. I had asked her to teach me what she knew, and to help me become what I ought to be in art. Meanwhile, I was under the umbrella of my father's training in the dairy business. Both of these people, my Mom and Dad, endured many a frustrated hour in the process of imparting what they knew to their stiff-necked son. I, too, was eager to teach the world how to do it right. Now, looking back at forty-five, I cringe at my arrogance, and wild-eyed lack of informed judgment.

But it was a journey of learning, and I never lost sight of the fact that I had been placed in my mother's womb by a Potter, one who uses nothing to make something. (I, of course, use something to make something. In that respect there is a vast difference.) I had been taught, or had learned, that if you are going to bow to someone, bow low.

So I did.

To Mom.

To Dad.

To Him.

But in hindsight I can think of myself only as an impossible student.

My life can be reduced to an issue of love. All that I am, and all that I know (if indeed, either are worthy of comment) I owe to a few single human beings who loved me. Why would they love someone so incorrigible?

So insensitive?

So improbable to make it out of the prison of his history and thoughts?

The answer to that question can only be this: I don't know.

But they did.

I owe it all to a few who were willing to believe in me. They saw past my failures to something else. They saw what I could not.

There was David

and Wayne

and Danny

Bruce,

There was Tom and Carolyn,
    and Chuck…
just a handful.

But, I am what I am because of their love. They were all willing to lose me by telling me the truth.

Through them I learned the truth…and that it brings liberty.
Freedom.
The blessed joy of life.

Through these people I learned that one person can make a transformation, a transformation that is total and complete. A complete turnaround.
All it takes is one.
It was Mother Teresa, whom I have never quite understood, but whom I have always listened to, who said this: "If you can't feed the many, then just feed one."
And, I, the one that was fed, will be forever different.

"You will say I am old and mad, but I answer that there is no better way of keeping sane and free from anxiety than being mad."
— MICHELANGELO

But, over the years I have tried to imagine what it would be like to be without that kind of help. The painter, or the artist, is on a crazy journey to himself. It is true that "once you can see what you can do, you can find out who you are." The pain and lonesomeness of getting to a thousand works, not to mention five thousand, and all the while paying your bills by the fruit of your hands, is no small task.

My heart goes out to people like me.

That is, of course, why I started writing letters to my students when I commenced this journey. If someone like me can do it, anyone can. But even more, I know what it is like to need a hand and get one.

What if you need a hand and don't get one?
That has never happened to me. So I have been given much. If I have been given much I owe much.
I owe you the truth.
I owe you my honesty.
I owe you my hand.

Until we meet face-to-face, and smile, and spit into the wind together, this book will have to do.

I am in the grip of a wonderful madness. It was brought on by love. I am now a horse of a different color.

I invite you, with all my heart, to become one, too.

—W. H.

CREDIT TO WHOM CREDIT IS DUE

It goes three ways:

FIRST, to my Sweetheart of twenty-one years,
      who is everything I am not.
      Kay Konze Herring

SECOND, to my Dad of forty-five years,
      whose patience with me was immense.
      Henry Philip Herring

THIRD, to my Leader of twenty-four years,
      who personally died for my sins.
      Jesus of Nazareth

PLUS, of course, credit goes to my daughters:
      Carolyn Charlese
      Kindra Jolynn
      Joanna Christine
      Teresa Dawn...
         the four lights of my life

A WORD OF THANKS

Because she:

• went through the agony of my birth
at noon on the 18th of February, 1948
• changed my diapers
• prayed with me next to my bed
• fed me with her dreams
• and even welcomed me back
after I hurt her so much,

and because she taught me
without spoiling me,

I offer this word of thanks to
Janet May Herring,
my mentor, and
my mother.

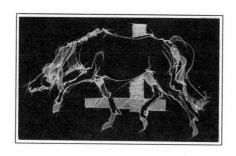

I dedicate this book
to my students,
especially
the
dark horses
who were told
they
would never win.

*"A dark horse,
which had never been thought of...
rushed past the grandstand
to sweeping triumph."*

— BENJAMIN DISRAELI
"The Young Duke"

A EULOGY
AN ENCOMIUM
A PANEGYRIC

HOWEVER it is said, I cannot release this book to you unless I pay tribute to those whom I saw from a window of the jet.

It was an early morning in January.

Cold. Wet. Cloudy.

But they were there, and they lifted their hands, waving, to get my attention.

They said, **"Do it for us, Bill."**

It was my imagination.

I was flying the Delta Shuttle out of Washington National. As the jet rose above the nerve center of the world, there they were. All standing on their grave stones, looking up at me from their military arrangement in Arlington National Cemetery.

I knew what they meant when they signaled me. There were hundreds of them.

I know about them.

They know about me.

They are the ones who cannot speak.

I am the one who can.

ONLY a few months before, with small flags adorning the memory of each of their offerings, I met many of them. It was 5–26–92, Memorial Day.

> I met Larry E. Smedley
> Medal of Honor
> CPL
> March 4, 1949
> December 21, 1967

I met Henry P. Russell
    Medal of Honor
    Captain
    United States Army
    Spanish American War
    June 10, 1878
    December 1, 1956

I met John Coughlin
    Medal of Honor
    Brevet Brigadier General
    United Sates Volunteer
    May 20, 1912

One had died in battle in Vietnam at the age of 18.
Two died of natural causes.
But all three put their lives on the line, and did it with class.
    One paid early.
    Two paid later.

But among those I met was one who touched me more deeply. He was born five days before I was, and was killed in Vietnam while I was in my fourth year of the Cadet Corps at Texas A&M. It was not his name, rank or date of death that got to me, although I would never have let him in so far to my heart if we were not born so close together. He was more like the rest of them there, all dead, and without the Medal of Honor.
    It was what he left me on the stone:

    Mark A. Whikehart
    Warrant Officer
    United States Army
    February 13, 1948 - March 17, 1970
    Vietnam
"For those who have fought for it,
Freedom is a taste the protected will never know."

I am one of the protected ones.
I will never know what he knew.
Indeed I never met him.

    He, and they, the ones who were waving at me,
    did it for me.
    So, I waved back, and I was moved to tears.
    And I said to them, **"Count on it."**

                — W. H.

"*THE American eagle*
sits on his perch,
a large, strong bird
with formidable beak and claws.
There he sits motionless
and M. Gromyko
[Soviet delegate to the U.N.]
is sent day after day
to prod him
with a sharp pointed stick —
now his neck,
now under his wings,
now his tail feathers.
All the time
the eagle keeps quite still.
But it would be
a great mistake to suppose
that nothing is going on
inside the breast of the eagle."

— WINSTON CHURCHILL
House of Commons
July 5, 1946

THE WHITE SIDE OF A DARK ISSUE...

THE PURPOSE OF A BOOK

"How many a young man has dated a new era in his life from the reading of a book. The book exists for us perchance which will explain our miracles and reveal new ones. The at present unutterable things we may find somewhere uttered. These same questions that disturb and puzzle and confound us have in their turn occurred to all the wise men; not one has been omitted; and each has answered them according to his ability, by his words, and his life."

— HENRY DAVID THOREAU
Born 1817
Dead at 45 near Walden Pond, Massachusetts
Author and Naturalist
American

"WHY DO I WRITE?
I write to entertain my friends and to exasperate my enemies.
To unfold the folded lie, to record the truth of our time,
and, of course, to promote esthetic bliss."

— EDWARD ABBEY
Born 1927
Dead at 62 in Oracle, Arizona
Author and Naturalist
American

"A life passed among pictures
makes not a painter
— else the policeman in the National Gallery
might assert himself."

— JAMES ABBOTT MCNEILL WHISTLER
The Gentle Art of Making Enemies

SOME TIPS
ON AVOIDING
AN OVER-STRESSED STATE

SOME stress is necessary. One educator recently told me that he felt his students needed a certain "level of discomfort that was necessary for production."

Where, then, can you find that magical "level"? One former college student I know developed severe hypoglycemia as a result of the stress generated in pursuit of a double degree in Medicine and Biology in four years.

Too much is bad.

Too little is bad.

No, I do not have the answer to finding the magical amount.

But, I do know that some people manage stress better than others....

WHAT, then, are some tips for managing stress from an artist's point of view? I can think of three.

ONE: *If at all possible, get your first thousand paintings done before you must depend upon sales to support you.* To rush into the marketplace without the confidence produced by having made thousands of mistakes will probably produce excess stress.

TWO: *Get your marriage squared away before you start gambling.* Do not ever conclude that the expression of your gift is more important than your role as a father, or as a husband. Your kids will not remember you for your artwork...but for your *home*work.

THREE: *Remember there is always room at the top.* I recently read that there are 183,682 people like me at work in America. Don't let that competition stress you out.

NOBODY CAN COMPETE WITH
A GENUINE GIFT
FROM GOD.

—W. H.

ON ART ASSOCIATIONS

IT goes without saying that
you should avoid them at all costs.
Why?

SIMPLE answer:
You usually can't afford it. There are
three things that you cannot afford:

ONE: **You can't afford to get involved in**
petty politics. For example, when I was asked
to head up our local association, I decided to
visit a painting session at a local ranch. When I
went out of my way to meet a couple I didn't know
(which I customarily do anyway), the woman made some
stupid remark about the fact that I was now "campaigning." I didn't
know her from Adam (and certainly not Eve). It was all I could do to
contain myself. If you decide to get involved in a local association, you
had better decide if you can afford such innuendos on your character.
To do any public thing these days includes the idea that everyone
thinks you have base motives.

TWO: **You can't afford the competition.** Not that you care to
compete against living people…but you will do it anyhow. That's
what regional awards are all about. The professional artist cares only
about National, or International, awards, if he cares at all. He should
be in competition with Rubens, not his contemporaries. But, if you get
involved locally, you will want to participate. If you participate in a show,
you had better exclude yourself from judging. You cannot afford the little ego
games if you don't.

THREE: **You can't afford the time.** You see, most artists have enough of a hard time
painting, anyway. Unless you have done your first thousand paintings, you have no
business spending time in some other little good thing. Good things probably *already*
eat up your painting time. Your great priority is production.

IF you have time to spare, ignore this point.

—W. H.

ON HIGH PERFORMANCE

Two days ago I listened to A&M "whup up" on Houston. Great football game! At half time, during one of the advertising "blurbs," I heard that the Aggies had more National Merit Scholars than any other school in the country. Impressive!

My mind went back to 1971. I was in my last of a five year hitch at College Station. For several months I had been developing an appreciation for a sophomore named Bob Woody. Frankly, he astounded me.

He was: organized, but seemed spontaneous;

intense, but not exhausted;

broadminded, yet limited in his activities;

well-liked, but a loner;

a team man, but very individualistic;

had a 4.0 grade average (no buts);

a "Presidential Scholar," no less;

Pre-Med.

ONE day he gave me a painting— men in a boat at sea. He had that *look* in his eye— a sparkle. It was almost like that of a little boy who had found a lost marble. His excitement was really contagious. Really!

Everyone admired him, and we all wanted to know his secrets.

One day I wandered in and sat down. As usual he didn't have that "blurry-eyed look of lostness" that most "Aggies" live with on a daily level. He just sat back, smiled, and asked, "What's on your mind?"

"How do you do it?" I inquired. "How do you keep all you do in balance? I admire you. Tell me your secrets!"

He laughed, then looked at me with that beam in his eye. He said, "It's simple. I get at least eight hours of sleep each night, and I follow the direction of my natural interests."

I waited for more...in vain.

1. Get plenty of sleep.
2. Follow the direction of your natural interests.

OVER the years, I have come to realize he was right.

—W. H.

"TIRED *officers are always pessimists.*"

— GENERAL GEORGE PATTON
from *Patton: Ordeal and Triumph*
by Ladislas Farago

ON DREAMING

*If you could have a dream come true,
who would you most want to paint like?*

*If you could borrow from the past,
what would you want the most?*

Here's my list:

FROM THE MASTERS:
The economy of line like Guardi.
The majesty of many figures in space like Canaletto.
The compositional ideas of Degas.
To draw like Rubens.
To render clothing like Rembrandt.
The colors of Tiepolo.
The line of Toulouse-Lautrec.
The magic of Venice like Turner.
To paint animals like Gainsborough.
The endurance of Monet.
To treat light on the figure like Renoir.
Freeness of mind like Whistler.
The taste of Vermeer.
Sensitivity to the human form like Van Dyke.
To paint horses like Delacroix.
The brush stroke of Frans Hals.
The fantastic flair of Fechin.

FROM CONTEMPORARIES:
To handle paint like Bob Peak.
The wonderful sloppiness of Reid.
The standing figures of Robert E. Wood.
Open color like Neiman.
The flowers of Jan Herring.
The audacity of R. C. Gorman.

WHAT I COULD DO WITHOUT:
Cezanne altogether.
All of Picasso's periods.
New York City.

— W. H.

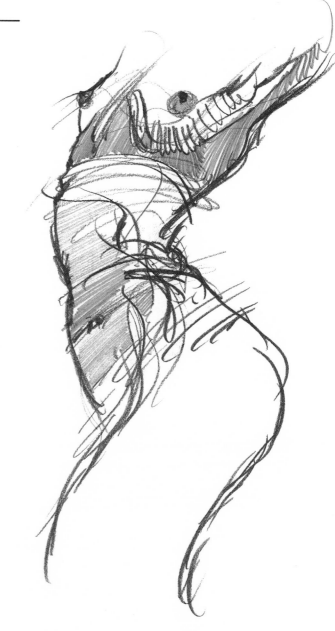

*"In the entire history of art there is not
a single painter
whose spontaneous brush-strokes
show greater infallibility."*

— **FREDERICK TAUBES**
Anatomy of Genius
Speaking of Frans Hals

ON FLIGHTS FROM REALITY

ARE you a dangerous person?
Are you sure that you are thinking correctly?
Have you taken a "flight from reality"?

To help ask and answer the question, allow me to refer to the chronicles of Albert Speer. *He was the **artist** that followed another **artist** into near oblivion.* He was the "straight thinking architect" who bought into the plans and lifestyle of a dynamic leader named Adolf Hitler. Hitler's own "flight from reality" was way too costly to ever forget. Catch a glimpse of his thinking from his best friend's pen:

"Hitler predicted that a war with the Soviet Union would be *child's play*. He clung to the end to his preconceived opinion that the troops of the western countries were *poor fighting material*. He was convinced that democracy *"feebled"* a nation. As late as the summer of 1944 he held to his theory that all the ground that had been lost in the west would be *quickly "reconquered."* His opinions on the western statesmen had a similar bias. He considered *Churchill,* as he often stated during the situation conferences, an *incompetent, alcoholic demagogue.* He also asserted in all seriousness, that *Roosevelt* was not a victim of infantile paralysis but of syphilitic paralysis and was therefore *mentally unsound.* These opinions, too, were indications of his flight from reality in the last years of his life."

My point? I do not want to say that all artists are gullible, or that they tend to all fly in unreal worlds, but the two artists mentioned above got a lot of people into serious trouble. (Hitler had three paintings showing in Paris during his stay in Vienna.)

And so will you if you tend to take "flights from reality." You see, *you are responsible for how you think.* Nobody, even an "eccentric artist," has the right to go wrong in the areas of serious human interest.

Better check yourself out. Too many dumb ideas may cost you more than you think.

It's a good time to question your answers.

— W. H.

P.S. I guess all this was prompted by a really strange mind I met recently. It made me seriously reconsider my flight plans. One of the two of us needs help!

ON BREAKING THE MOLD

FEELING pressure to be normal?
Are you often influenced by what people think about you?

ARE you intimidated by the look of another person who thinks that you are out to lunch?
Think about this:
1. High levels of creativity are linked to high amounts of extra available energy.
2. High levels of extra available energy are linked to having fun.
3. High levels of fun are linked to being a kid.
4. Being like a kid means that you run with the moment...
   jump with the bounce...
   stay up 'til you conk out...
   follow your curiosity...
   laugh out loud...
   act on impulse...
   are spontaneous...
   are out for fun...
   because life is something to be explored.
5. Energy levels have little to do with how much sleep you get.

So, maybe you have gotten the impression that the child in you is supposed to be grown up. The Puritans believed that also. They maintained that having pleasure and being spontaneous were definite sins. (Thank God the Victorians are gone, too.)
Just blow all that off.
Your difference is what makes you special, and if others think you don't fit the mold...just increase their blood pressure by stomping that mold under your feet in an act of

         supreme
             childish
                 pleasure.

If that kid in you ever dies, you've had it. When life isn't fun anymore, you've lost touch with it. The only thing to do is . . .
        BREAK THE MOLD.
Sound like fun? It is!
Normal people aren't normal...if you know what I mean.

                —W. H.

> *"I believe the more you are like society, the less you impact it."*
>
> — HOWARD HENDRICKS

A NEW SPELLING DICTIONARY

Anonymous donor for the purpose of promoting irrational, open-mouthed laughter:

AEROPALMICS
(ayr o palm' iks)
n. The study of wind resistance conducted by holding a cupped hand out the car window.

AQUADEXTROUS
(ak wa deks' trus)
adj. Possessing the ability to turn the bathtub faucet on and off with your toes.

AQUALIBRIUM
(ak wa lib' re um)
n. The point where the stream of drinking fountain water is at its perfect height, thus relieving the drinker from (a) having to suck the nozzle, or (b) squirting himself in the eye.

LACTOMANGULATION
(lak' to man gyu lay' shun)
adv. Manhandling the "open here" spout on a milk carton so badly that one has to resort to using the "illegal" side.

PSYCHOPHOBIA
(sy ko fo' be uh)
n. The compulsion when using a host's bathroom to peer behind the shower curtain and make sure no one is waiting for you.

TELECRASTINATION
(tel a kras tin ay' shun)
n. The act of always letting the phone ring at least twice before you pick it up, even when you're only six inches away.

TELEPRESSION
(tel e pre' shun)
n. The deep-seated guilt which stems from knowing that you did not try hard enough to "look up the number on your own" and instead put the burden on the directory assistant.

DECLARATION OF INDEPENDENCE

*"I
no
longer
choose
to be
a silver sphere
in
life's
pin ball game
being
pushed
into
satisfying goals
I
did not choose
— nor scoring points
for
another's
benefit."*

— P. S. JOHNSON

WARNING

WHEN I am an old woman I shall wear purple
With a red hat which doesn't go, and doesn't suit me,
And I shall spend my pension on brandy and summer gloves
And satin sandals, and say we've no money for butter.
I shall sit down on the pavement when I'm tired
And gobble up samples in shops and press alarm bells
And run my stick along the public railings
And make up for the sobriety of my youth.
I shall go out in my slippers in the rain
And pick the flowers in other people's gardens
And learn to spit.

— JENNY JOSEPH

♥

ON *the back of a T-shirt*
worn by a cat:

"**I**'M
STUPID
AND
I
HATE
YOU
—
FEED
ME!"

AWKWARD TEENAGE
HORSE WAITING FOR
HIS VOICE TO
CHANGE

ON PLANNING

*"**T**HERE are so many more possibilities that something
other than what we expected and hoped for will happen,
that the probability of things happening our way is remote."*

I like that.
The quote comes from a book on management I have been reading…and really hits
the snake in the mouth.

The snake needs to be hit in the mouth…otherwise it bites.

It always bites.

Life bites.

Bit by bit.

What is terribly important is learning the art of keeping a correct perspective. Pressure
doesn't change you…it reveals you. Nothing is more healthy than believing that what
comes your way is by design…that you are on schedule…and that the one doing the
biting is **not a snake**.

—W. H.

ON BUILDING
A REPUTATION

"WILLIAM HENRY PICKERING (1858-1938) discovered Phoebe, the ninth and most distant moon of the planet Saturn. He made observations of the planet Mars from a branch of Harvard's observatory that he and his brother had established at Arequipa, Peru."

—NEW STANDARD ENCYCLOPEDIA, Volumn 13
Standard Education Corporation, Chicago, 1981

ARE you impressed?
Does it matter to you who he was?
Or what he did?

Not to me. I could care less, and most everyone could care less about you.

If you are betting that your importance will come from the chronicles of men as they record your life in their volumes of encyclopedias, forget it. You have got to live for something more than that. What other men think about you matters **not one flip**.

Got any answers? Maybe you ought to ask some of the right questions. Your inspiration will depend on it!

— W. H.

❖

"AND I think it's down to you finally
— whether you want to do something…
What you're after…
What you're going for…
And anyway, you have to get behind yourself.
And you have to get behind anyone else
who's doing anything of worth.
There's altogether too little of that."

— ANGELICA HOUSTON
Washington Post
Sunday, November 17, 1991

"WHEN I look around
and see what robots
the American people are,
it really scares
the shit out of me."

— MARK BAKER
Nam

EVEN THE ANIMALS RUN
FROM DEMS DUALE.

QUESTION:

What is it like to be an artist?

"IT is like
a great blaze in your soul,
and nobody ever comes to heat himself by it.
The passers-by just see a little smoke,
there at the top,
coming out of the chimney,
and walk on."

"I feel in myself a fire
which I cannot let die out;
on the contrary
I must quicken it,
although
I don't know where this
will lead me."

— VINCENT

"Writing songs is why I'm here…
Every time I hold that pencil, Lord,
Would you kindly hold my hand."

—Larry Gatlin
"Songwriter's Trilogy"
1980, CBS Inc.

ARE YOU LOOKING
AT THE MODEL?

*From the Hacienda Hotel, next to
the Iglesia de Santa Prisca, Taxco, Mexico*

I find it amusing when people gather around when I am drawing. Really, they have no idea that what I'm doing anyone can do.

For example, this morning a Mexican male sauntered up to Billy, my apprentice for the trip, and commented to his friend: "Come see, he is doing this with his eye alone. How beautiful!" "Gee," I said to myself, "if he only knew how simple this is to do if properly taught."

I again think of the importance of two issues in a person's beginnings:

1. *Train the eye to see.* Make your eye travel over the surface of anything at one slow pace. Most of our eyes already know how to dance…few know how to crawl.

2. *Train the hand to follow.* If you can see it, you must train you hand to record it. People are amazed when you draw while not looking at the paper. They should be amazed if they see you do otherwise.

— W. H.

ON THE INFLUENCE OF IDEAS

*Tell me, where do ideas come from?
How are they born?*

A week ago I was discussing similar things with another artist, at which point he mentioned that he had seen a revolutionary change come over his son. The change, which ultimately meant graduating *suma cum laude* in Geo-physics, came about when "the boy was transferred to a private school where the other students discussed IDEAS."

I suggest to you that there are three levels of candid conversation which reveal a person's way of mental life:

Level One: Mostly discuss **people**

Level Two: Mostly discuss **events**

Level Three: Mostly discuss **ideas**

I**f**
you are
not
on level three,
get there.

— W. H.

*"Children are not only interested,
they are prepared to be vitally touched
by the great things of life."*

—Carol Bly
"Growing Up Expressive"
Letters from the Country

ON GIFTEDNESS

Do you believe giftedness can be passed on by people? I do.

I have been touched afresh by the impact of certain people on Michelangelo's life. When he was just thirteen, one year before starting a serious apprenticeship of seven years, he had the unspeakable privilege of walking around his home town and seeing— out in the open— what I hope to see even once in my lifetime.

1. He saw two sets of doors, located at churches not far from where he lived, that had taken one man 45 years to create. His name was Ghiberti. They were called the Gates of Paradise; of pure gold. A picture of these doors almost makes you cry— and young Michelangelo could sit in front of them hours upon end. And did.

2. Then, about 64 years before Michelangelo was born, the very great sculptor, Donatello, did a free-standing marble sculpture for the Guild of Flax Merchants in Florence, Italy. Michelangelo visited this work often. It was a sculpture of St. Mark…and he was so touched by the work that he later wrote: "It would have been impossible to reject the Gospel preached by such a straight-forward man as this."

3. Finally, *that* year, when he was thirteen (1488), the man died who had done the other landmark piece of art that was to greatly mold his mind: Verrocchio. It was a small, free-standing bronze of a child holding a dolphin. Verrocchio finished it in 1475, the year Michelangelo was born.

These three men became very important to Michelangelo as you put them into perspective:

Ghiberti taught Donatello;
Donatello taught Verrocchio;
Bertoldo di Giovanni was taught by all three,
and it was this man, Bertoldo, who was to be Michelangelo's mentor.

The gifts of these men were deposited to Michelangelo's account…by Bertoldo…and daily he could go see what they had done…

done in one town,
at one time in history,
for all to see…
especially him.

And how about you? What treasures have been passed on to you by gifted people? It is time to decide:

Rembrandt decided at **twelve**;
Renoir decided at **thirteen**.

How old are you?

— W. H.

"**D**EGAS *encouraged me*
by saying the work I
had done this summer was not bad.
HOW *much I*
would like to believe it!"

— TOULOUSE-LAUTREC

ON THE THREE THINGS YOU NEED TO BECOME GREAT

THREE things are necessary to be a great painter. However, the mere presence of these qualities is no guarantee whatsoever that it will happen.

Let me illustrate by quoting some lines from the biography of a person named Floda Reltih. You will see that these qualities were clearly well intact at an early age...yet *I know* that *you know* that you have never heard of this person in discussions about the masters.

THOSE three things. What are they?

ONE: *A clear sense of destiny...an understanding that you were born for it.*

"...I developed a plan of my own...and this occurred at the early age of twelve. How it happened, I, myself, do not know, but one day it became clear to me that I would become a painter, an artist."

TWO: *A keen understanding of what one does **not** want to do.*

"All attempts on my father's part to inspire me with love or pleasure in his profession by stories from his own life accomplished the exact opposite. I yawned and grew sick to my stomach at the thought of sitting in an office, deprived of my liberty; ceasing to be master of my own time and being compelled to force the content of a whole life into blanks that had to be filled out."

Also, "My father forbade me to nourish the slightest hope of ever being allowed to study art. I went one step further and declared that if that was the case, I would stop studying all together."

"My conviction grew stronger and stronger....The fact that by this time my gift for drawing had been recognized in school made my determination all the firmer. Neither pleas nor threats could change it one bit. I wanted to become a painter...."

THREE: *A high resolve that endures suffering in its quest for the best...an indomitable will.*

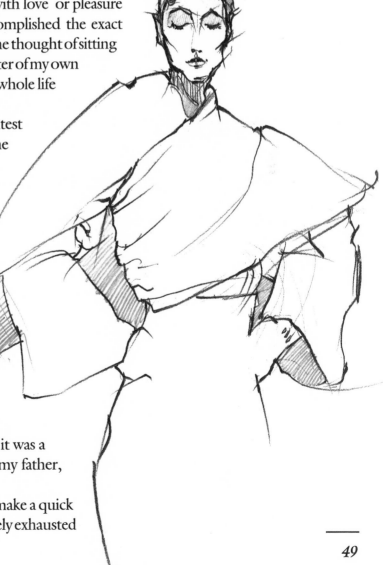

"The death of my mother put a sudden end to all my high flown plans. It was the conclusion of a long and painful illness, which, from the beginning left little hope of recovery. Yet it was a dreadful blow, particularly for me. I had honored my father, but my mother I had loved."

"Poverty and hard reality now compelled me to make a quick decision. What little my father had left had been largely exhausted by my mother's grave illness; the orphan's pension to which I was entitled was not enough for me to live on, and so I was faced with the problem of somehow making my own living."

"In my hand a suitcase full of clothes and underwear; in my heart an indomitable will…. I, too, hoped to wrest from Fate what my father had accomplished fifty years before; I, too, wanted to become 'something'…."

Yes, this individual had *those three things* that are most necessary to become a great artist: **He knew** *Fate had chosen him for it.*

He knew *what he did* **not** *want to be.*

He knew *he could* **not** *let becoming an orphan at fifteen stop him.*

The right stuff. He had it, but it didn't get *him* there. Have you ever seen any of Floda's drawings? Having *those three things* doesn't guarantee that I will see any of *your* drawings either. Life is tricky!

I<small>F</small> you don't believe me, spell the artist's name backwards.

—W. H.

"W<small>ITH</small> one stroke you have
transformed the state of my soul.
That in the hour of her deepest need Germany
gives birth to a Hitler proves her vitality;
as do the influences that emanate from him;
for these two things— personality and influence—
belong together… may God protect you!"

— S<small>IR</small> N<small>EVILLE</small> C<small>HAMBERLAIN</small>
   from a letter to Hitler
   The Rise and the Fall of the Third Reich

"I think I shall succeed because I want to write!"

April 4th

"You've known for a long time that my greatest wish is to become a journalist someday and later on a famous writer. Whether these leanings toward greatness (or insanity?) will ever materialize remains to be seen..."

May 11th

"That's the difficulty in these times: ideals, dreams, and cherished hopes rise within us, only to meet the horrible truth and be shattered."

July 15th

"I...keep trying to find a way of becoming what I would so like to be, and what I could be, if...there weren't any other people living in the world."

The last sentence written on the day of the raid, August 4, 1944

— Anne Frank

"**L**ISTENING.
A very dangerous thing.
If one listens
one may be convinced."
— OSCAR WILDE

FINDING THE GIFTED CHILD

I have been given the task of developing a test for giftedness in the visual arts. The target area involves the seventh and eighth graders in our local school district.

Eleven schools. How do I do it?

What marks am I looking for? What makes one kid stand out over another? What is the one recognizable factor that brands the gifted child?

FIRST, I must recognize some general realities, such as:

1. Children tend to develop interests in the same areas of interest that their parents maintain. *Kids will be like their parents.*

2. *The greatest evidence of a gift is a strong desire that will not go away.* Interest of high intensity is a sure mark.

3. *Some gifted children are not teachable in the area of their interest.* It will not even appear, perhaps, 'til their twenties. If the child is strong-willed, first-born, male, and at odds with parental authority…it (the gift) may be hidden under the skin.

4. *Many gifted kids* (in visual arts) *would not be caught dead in an art class.* The reason? Still too much hangover from the Sixties: eccentric looking teachers; emphasis on creativity rather than mastery of the basics (like drawing).

5. *Many boys perceive art as either a woman's world, or a homosexual's world.* Woman's because of the women-oriented art clubs, art associations, workshops, etc., and homosexual—well, for example, the first two male artists I met were "gay."

6. *Many girls raised in the Southwest perceive art as a male world* because prominent artists of renown are 99% male in the "western art" game. Also, the "farm concept" of a woman does not usually include art as something to major in…but, rather, something to tinker with— a nice hobby.

7. It goes without saying that *a child will not tend to get hold of his purpose 'til he grabs hold of his maker.* If genuine communication has not been established, giftedness usually remains *out of focus.* It is in the period of "this wrestling" that a child is subject to many false or counterfeit signals. Some heed the wrong drummer.

To find a gifted child, then, I must remember at least seven areas of plain reality:

1. The tremendous impact of parents.
2. There must be a strong desire.
3. The child must be teachable.
4. Negative influence of the Sixties.
5. Wrong male perceptions.
6. Wrong female perceptions.
7. "Drummer" problems.

In spite of all that…or in light of all that…
I trust that I will be directed to some special hungry hearts.
There is usually smoke where there is fire.

—W. H.

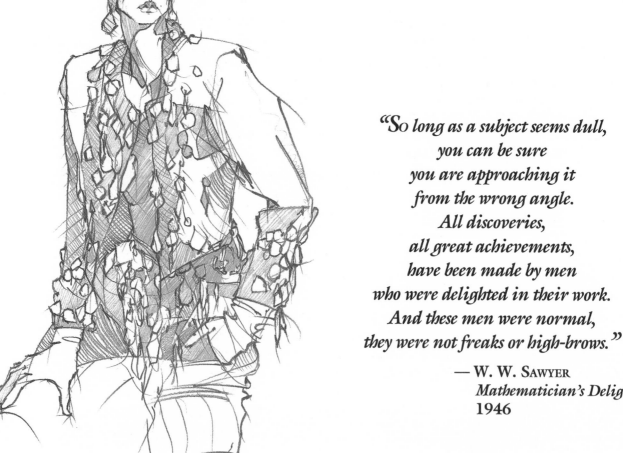

"So long as a subject seems dull,
you can be sure
you are approaching it
from the wrong angle.
All discoveries,
all great achievements,
have been made by men
who were delighted in their work.
And these men were normal,
they were not freaks or high-brows."

— W. W. SAWYER
Mathematician's Delight
1946

"Too often, unfortunately, teaching seems to proceed on the philosophy that adults have to do dull jobs, and that children should get used to dull work as quickly as possible. The result is an entirely justified hatred and contempt for all kinds of learning and intellectual life."

— W. W. Sawyer
Mathematician's Delight
1946

WHY YOU CAN'T TRUST NEW ART BOOKS & OLD ART TEACHERS

NEXT to my own trash can out front, there is more raw garbage in art books than anywhere else. I'll take that back. The real garbage award should go to the eastern art critics…or should it go to the college art professors?

As usual, I am confused.

Who did it?
How pervasive is it?
How can we stop it?

Among the top awards in this category, one should go to the idiot who came up with the idea found in one of the latest new art books that "spontaneity is more important to the creative process than technique." I run into this all the time, in three ways:

1. *American artists, in general, do not want technique— they want innovation.* Skipping over the issue of mastering the basic things is in vogue. For example, it is almost below the mentality of today's artist to start at the beginning. Offer a class on the basic techniques of watercolor, and what do you get? Yet, the weakness that is crippling the artists I know is this — they do not habitually practice the basic techniques:

A. Like pure contour drawing.
B. Modified contour drawing.
C. The quick flash gesture.
D. Like doing a simple one color graded wash.
E. Learning to lose an edge.
F. Cushioning values.

2. *The second way I run into it is by observing old art teachers.* (Thank God for the exception to what I will now mention.) If the student asks the teacher if they ever did "pure contour drawing," the answer is usually something like "Oh, yes, I've been doing that all my life."

Well, a casual observer (i.e. the student who asked the question) could draw the following conclusions:

ONE. Pure contour drawing is the hardest discipline on earth with regard to learning to draw. If the teacher says she has been doing it all her life, then this teacher must be very disciplined. But the truth is that she hasn't; she thinks now that "such basic things" are for the younger kids, and it would be below her to admit that it was important for her now.

TWO. The kid can see that the teacher draws like a third grader…and she just said she had been doing contour drawing all her life…and it is therefore obvious to him that this kind of drawing does not help at all.

What happened here is this: the kid thinks the teacher is telling the truth about the "all of her life" bit. He reacts toward discipline in basic drawing techniques the same way the young boy reacts toward the Bible when his recently divorced dad tells him he's been "studying the Bible all his life."

Failure to master the basic techniques while you are young will force you to trivialize them when you are older, turn you into a liar and a ruiner of kids.

3. *Thirdly, I run into the idea of "spontaneity vs. technique" when I read about the thinking of the masters.* Now don't jump to conclusions! What I mean is this: the masters generally thought otherwise. When they say so, they create an impact using contrast — between what they say, and what I see. In other words, the more I read of their thinking, the more I see how insane we have become.

Let me quote "The Great Romantic," Eugene Delacroix, who wrote in his journal the statement that set me off on this tirade in the first place: "Technique must be perfected until it never obtrudes on the final effect of spontaneity."

In other words, the really great performers in any endeavor are the ones who have mastered the basic moves so well that they appear to be spontaneous. You will never create anything of note if you do not learn the basic techniques…and practice them over and over 'til you die. *They must never be below you!*

— W. H.

*"As a rule,
someone who has difficulty with painting
in any medium
is not prepared to believe that
the real trouble is
ignorance of
drawing and composition."*

— W. H.

"I am horribly depressed at the moment.
Its always the same
— work that's so hard and uncertain.
I am *so slow*.
When will I achieve
a more rapid way of painting?
…Oh, Fantin, I know so little."

— WHISTLER
Letter to Fantin-Latour in Paris, 1864
Whistler had just turned 30 years old

WHETHER IT IS BETTER TO DRAW IN COMPANY OR NOT

"I say and insist that drawing in company is much better than alone, for many reasons. The first is that you would be ashamed of being seen among a number of draughtsmen if you are weak, and this feeling of shame will lead you to good study; secondly a wholesome envy will stimulate you to join the number of those who are more praised than you are, for the praise of others will spur you on; yet another is that you can learn from the drawings of those that do better than yourself; and if you are better than the others, you can profit by your contempt for their defects, and the praise of others will incite you to further efforts."

— LEONARDO DA VINCI
The Artist's Life

"*THERE was a Texan striding along 57th Street in Manhattan who asked a stranger, 'Tell me, partner, how do I get to Carnegie Hall?' and the stranger replied, 'Practice, practice.'*"

— WILLIAM SAFIRE

DEFINING YOUR INTENT

YOU have two great choices.
You can go right.
Or you can go left.
But there are no other choices.

YOU either paint with a message or you don't.
If you have a message you are a commercial artist.
If you don't have a message you are a fine artist.

IT all depends on your intent.

IF you are bent toward a message, you will train one way. If you are bent to beauty, you will train in quite another manner, indeed. It is important to discuss this issue because of this disturbing fact: there are dozens of commercial artists teaching "fine art" workshops. They are giving the students commercial art rules in the name of "fine art," and many hungry hearts have been ill-touched by the resulting confusion.

The major point of confusion comes from a realization that the instructors don't have accurate definitions themselves, and therefore do this damage while they are well-meaning and attempting to help the student. For example, ninety-nine out of ninety-nine commercial artists believe this: commercial art is what you do for someone else and fine art is what you do for yourself, usually called easel painting. They firmly assert that commercial art is "lower" and fine art is "higher." They all seem to "live" for the day they can make their living doing "fine art."

But such an idea is sadly misplaced in the relationship to logic. Rather, both commercial art and fine art are separate and equal intents. Once a person is found to be bent one way, it is seldom and extremely rare to see him go the other. In other words, once a commercial artist, always a commercial artist, no matter who you are working for. And, to further juice-up the argument, there are two kinds of commercial artists, the sellers and the tellers. They are either bent to selling an idea or product, or they are bent to telling a story. *The intent is a reflection of the bent, and an artist is seldom bent two ways.*

The fine artist finds himself oriented toward the magnetic pole of beauty. At this location on the art map there is no need for a message. It is just beauty for the sake of beauty, period.

Finally, what is the difference between the commercial artist and the fine artist in terms of how they train? The following chart should help you to see the contrast:

COMMERCIAL ART	FINE ART
Purpose for the eye: to stop it where the message is, thus a need to have a center of interest and a focal point	*Purpose for the eye:* to keep it traveling because there is no message, just the beauty of the surface; therefore, no need for a center of interest and a focal point
Values: "contrasted" to stop the eye, especially placing the lightest light next to the darkest dark where the message is	*Values:* "cushioned" to travel the eye, no need for more than a one value difference between any object in the work
Light source: usually two or more, preferably exotic	*Light source:* usually one source only, preferably classic
Choice of subject matter: extraordinary, sentimental and regional	*Choice of subject matter:* ordinary, in an attitude of repose, and universal
Use of color: strongest color in one quarter of the painting	*Use of color:* each color used in at least three of the four quarters
Purpose of color: to evoke a mood to match the message, usually illustrative and descriptive	*Purpose of color:* to create rhythm inside the picture plane, usually expressive and not descriptive
Purpose of a title: essential, is the key to understanding the message	*Purpose of a title:* not essential, for there is no door that needs a key
Purpose of the painting: to communicate	*Purpose of the painting:* to decorate

IT is my hope, then, that you, the student, learn to derive correct definitions, locate your intent, and train accordingly.

You will not be able to change how the teacher teaches, but you should know what they mean by what they say, even if *they* don't.

WITH all due respect—

W. H.

"THE great heresy in art is the teaching of a lesson."

— EDGAR ALLEN POE

*"The aim of painting
is not to create
an anecdotal fact,
but
a pictorial fact."*
— Braque

❖

*"A person looking at a picture
should be moved to exclaim,
'How beautiful!' rather than 'How true!'"*
— James McNeil Whistler

"PERHAPS the most bewildering belief reflecting raw human stupidity is this:
'beauty is in the eye of the beholder.'
Beauty exists whether a person has the eye to behold it or not.
That principle also applies to ugliness."

— W. H.

❖

"CHARACTER
contributes
to beauty.
It fortifies a woman
as her beauty fades.
A mode of conduct,
a standard of courage,
discipline, fortitude
and integrity
can do a great deal
to make
a
woman
beautiful."

— JACQUELINE BISSET
Quoted in *Los Angeles Times*

"OF THE CHOICE
OF BEAUTIFUL FACES"

"Look about you and take the best parts of many faces, of which
the beauty is established rather by public fame than by your own judgment;
for you may deceive yourself and select faces which bear resemblance
to your own…if you were ugly you would select faces that are not beautiful,
and you would then create ugly faces as many painters do.
For often a master's shapes resemble himself; so therefore select beauties
as I tell you and fix them in your mind."

— Leonardo Da Vinci
The Artist's Life

> *"We live by encouragement and die without it
> — slowly, sadly, angrily."*
> — CELESTE HOLM

FINDING A MENTOR

EVER heard of Carel Fabritius? He's probably not important to you. No big deal. But— have you heard of Rembrandt? "Of course," now you say.

You see, Carel Fabritius was killed in a huge explosion in Europe in 1654. He was only thirty-two years old. A painter. A student of Rembrandt. At the time of Carel's death, Rembrandt Harmenzoon Van Rijn was forty-eight years old. He would live to paint for fifteen more years.

Before he died, Carel Fabritius was to make a deposit in a man ten years younger than he was. His first name was Jan. Carel was his mentor. His "deposit" was what he had learned from Rembrandt.

TWO things stand out to me in this story.

ONE. There had never been anyone who could approximate the skill of Rembrandt until Fabritius came along. They seemed to paint alike. Fabritius never had time to take what he had learned into personal fruition. He never developed his own "style." He just did as Rembrandt did.

TWO. And "what he did" was passed on to Jan. This man, named Jan Vermeer was to take that "deposit" and turn it into gold. Nobody has ever painted the way he did. Nobody has ever touched him, and you do not see "Rembrandt" in his work anywhere.

Interestingly, Vermeer was never a mentor to anyone. He died at 43. Had eleven kids. Operated a frame shop. Died broke.

But, what I really had to say is this:
   A. It is impossible to be creative without mastering the basics.
   B. It is impossible to master the basics without a mentor.

I find these two points very critical these days because of current thinking patterns I encounter among the college grads in the art field.

THINKING PATTERN NUMBER ONE: "In art there are no such things as 'basics.' No rules. Whatever works for you is okay."

THINKING PATTERN NUMBER TWO: "I cannot afford to get around any one teacher. They might influence my own creativity. I have to do my own thing. I do not want to paint like someone else. I want to do something new."

MY ADVICE: Better look for a mentor. That person could be the key to *your* stardom. What if your mentor isn't a star? Ever heard of Pieter Lastman? No? He was Rembrandt's mentor. Lastman lived in Rembrandt's back yard. **Better take a look in yours.**

—W. H.

THE MENTOR

"I met a wise mentor today,
He encouraged me to think.
To find the answers inside myself.
So, I searched, experimented and hunted,
I peered into every corner within.
What I found were the answers I was seeking,
Lost amongst the clutter in my mind."

— JANE LEPPIN
Artist
Vienna, Virginia
(mother of twins)

"THERE are plenty of classy people out there
who want to help you.
Instead of waiting for someone to
take you under his wing,
go out and find a good wing to climb under."

— DAVE THOMAS
Founder of Wendys

A CHIMP NAMED
BUSTER LOOKING AT
THE PEOPLE LOOKING
AT HIM... THE ZOO

"YALE students were surveyed
about whom they admired most.
The top answer: NOBODY."

— Survey, *Life Magazine*
April 30, 1965

A FISH KNOWN AROUND
TOWN AS "LIPS"

"**LET** *early education*
be a form of amusement;
you will then be better able
to find out
the natural bent."

— PLATO
The Republic

ROOTS

*A root is something that attaches you to the earth,
and through which all nourishment finds its way to the leaves.
No roots, no life.*

Roots also keep you upright, especially in adverse weather.

How important, then, is it to search out your **human** roots?

My first known relative landed in Massachusetts as he concluded his journey from England; he was a preacher.

In my background I find politicians, even a three time candidate for the Presidency of the United States (Henry Clay). There is a famous baseball player (Mickey Mantle). There are doctors, more preachers, railroad workers and sheep ranchers. My grandfather homesteaded in Montana. I have in my roots a pianist and a dancer from New York. Some of my relatives ran a restaurant— and it was in that Ohio business establishment that my Daddy first met my Mother…which eventually led to me.

And I have one mysterious murder. Or, was it two?

In terms of towns and states, my roots run from Massachusetts to

> *Haver, Montana*
> *Great Falls, Montana*
> *Aberdeen, South Dakota*
> *Columbus, Ohio*
> *Worthington, Ohio*
> *Stuttgart, Arkansas*
> *Russelville, Kentucky*
> *Clint, Texas*

My great-grandfather Clayton Searle was a drummer boy in an Ohio regiment in the Civil War.

My Mother was in the Nurse's Corps, and worked in a Veteran's Hospital in Ohio in 1945…a ward nurse among WWII paraplegics.

My Daddy was a tail gunner in a B-25 in the South Pacific…sixty-six missions.

My Uncle was a survivor of the nightmare on Buna.

Of my Dad's two best friends, one was on Bataan, and the other flew multiple fighter missions over the English Channel at D-Day.

I am named for my Mother's brother Bill, killed at take-off while on duty flying the "Hump" in India during WWII. (I'll never forget seeing his gravestone in the "Punch Bowl" in Hawaii.)

On my wife's side are Germans— some of those who settled Texas:

> *Ranchers*
> *Dentists*
> *Army officers*
> *Oil business*

There are many alcoholics on both sides.
For sure, their genetics run through my system…and those of my kids.
A lot of who I am comes from my roots.

THERE are good roots.
There are bad roots.
Your leaves should tell the difference…
　　　'cause next comes the fruit.

　　　　　　　　— W. H.

*DID you know
that
Douglas MacArthur,
Franklin Delano Roosevelt
and
Winston Churchill
were
all
related?*

How Your Roots Can Hurt You

"A man lived by the side of the road and sold hot dogs.

He was hard of hearing so he had no radio.

He had trouble with his eyes so he read no newspapers.

But he sold good hot dogs.

He put up a sign on the highway telling how good they were.

Stood by the side of the road and cried: 'Buy a hot dog, Mister.'

And people bought.

He increased his meat and roll orders.

He bought a bigger stove to take care of his trade.

He got his son home from college to help him.

But then something happened...

His son said, 'Father, haven't you been listening to the radio?

If money stays 'tight', we are bound to have bad business.

There may be a big depression coming on.

You had better prepare for poor trade.'

Whereupon the father thought, 'Well, my son has been to college.

He reads the papers and he listens to the radio, and he ought to know.

So the father cut down on his meat and roll orders.

Took down his advertising signs.

And no longer bothered to stand on the highway to sell hot dogs.

And his hot dog sales fell almost overnight.

'You're right, son,' the father said to the boy.

'We are certainly headed for a depression.'"

— Anonymous

HOW YOUR ROOTS CAN HELP YOU

HANDED to me on a notecard
by a student in Houston:

*"**N**AVAJO Indians believe*
God is the only being
to create something that is perfect.
Therefore, in making their blankets,
the Navajos purposefully
put a mistake in every one."

SOUTHWESTERN
ELEGANCE...

ON FLYING BY YOURSELF

*How long does it take to be able
to do "your own thing" as a painter?
Go where you want. Paint what you want. Be on your own.*

I think it takes about two years.
Apparently, it takes the same time to learn to fly well on your own. Flying an airplane and painting a picture are similar. No, I don't fly, but let me give you a few statements by someone who did. Someone who spent a lot of time teaching others to fly.

He died twelve years before I was born. His name was Billy.

"Billy" was outspoken. That got him into a lot of trouble— demoted, in fact, from brigadier general to colonel. This man had commanded the largest air attack in WWI — 1,481 planes— during the St. Mihiel offensive of September, 1918. He was a forerunner, in spirit, of men like Gen. Douglas MacArthur and Gen. "Chesty" Puller. He dared to "tell it like it is." He dared to criticize his superiors.

In his case, Billy had a habit of going before Congress and publicly calling armed forces officials to the carpet. Specifically, after the wreck of the dirigible Shenandoah, Billy accused the army and navy of "incompetence, criminal negligence, and almost treasonable administration of the national defense." He was then court-martialed. He had warned of the chance of a Japanese attack on Pearl Harbor almost twenty years before it happened.

Eleven years after he died, Congressmen changed their minds…awarded him a special medal…and promoted him to major general, retroactive to the date of his death.

He was apparently one of the greatest "air minds" of all time.

A thinker…a teacher.

The year of his court-martial, 1925, he wrote a book entitled *Winged Defense*. It was that book I found in my attic. In that book, I believe, he gives a good description of what it takes to fly well…and if you use your imagination…what it takes to paint well.

LISTEN to his mind:

I believe it takes at least two years to make a suitable flying officer. You may teach a man to stagger around in the air in about three months. You may teach him to specialize in a given branch if he is an apt pupil in four or five months more; but to teach him every trick of the trade, to have confidence under all conditions, in the mountains, on the plains, over forests or over water, takes at least two years.

— Major General "Billy" Mitchell
Former Assistant Chief of the Air Force, U.S.A.

You must learn to fly alone. To paint by yourself…knowing what to do to keep it all going…is a magnificent feeling. Listen again to this aviator's description of a similar experience:

The first solo flight is the great event in a pilot's life. When he is removed from his instructor and takes the machine out alone, no matter how expert he may be, the feeling, that everything entirely depends upon him, with a new and strange apparatus in a medium in which he has never been used to doing things before, is appalling. He soon gets over it, however, and then begins flying across country, using his maps and landing in strange places.

Remember, the art of landing successfully in "strange places" takes a lot of work…and at least two years.

— W. H.

"The Wright Brothers didn't know any better, and taught the world to fly. Never forget that a man named Langley had a government contract at the time, but it took a couple of bicycle repairmen to teach the world to fly."

— Ross Perot

"It is much better to think of painting
(or the part of painting that you need to know)
as being half-a-dozen methods and twenty or so results,
of which you probably already know sixty percent.
I hope you are in the fortunate position
of never having been taught painting,
and therefore having no mistaken ideas about it."

— W. H.

FRANCIS BACON'S FAMOUS RULE FOR READING:

Read, not to contradict or confute,
nor to believe and take for granted,
nor to find talk and discourse,
but to weigh and consider.

Some books are to be tested,
others to be swallowed,
and some few to be chewed and digested.

ON GOADS AND NAILS

WHAT is the purpose of writing?

I think there are two:
ONE: *To act as a goad.* A goad is a pointed rod used to urge on an animal; a spur; a stimulus to action. It suggests a motive that keeps one going against one's will or desire; a spring; an impulse; an incentive; an inducement.

At the dairy operation I used to run, we often used cattle prods. Used properly, they can save a life. I often came to work and found one of our Holsteins who had just given birth laid out on the ground. Because of an imbalance in her calcium/phosphorous ratio, she would *not get up on her own.* This condition was called "milk fever." After trying to get up *just so many times,* she would become convinced she *couldn't.* The goad helped her to see the truth. If she failed to get up, she **never would again**. The cattle prod was an inducement to action. It is my belief that well-chosen, delightful words…will do the same: they will save a life.

TWO: *To serve the same purpose as a well-driven nail.* To "nail down" means to establish clearly and unmistakably; to fix; to fasten; to peg.

Yesterday my wife asked me to fix our screen. Mosquitoes were getting in through the hole…and big sore spots were all over the legs of my four daughters. When examining the screen, it became obvious to me that I had not nailed it down properly. I re-stretched the screen, and pounded in about twenty more nails to secure it unmistakably.

Similarly, many issues of our lives become "sore spots" when not "nailed down" properly. I believe that well-chosen, delightful words can serve the same purpose as a well-driven nail. To peg. To secure. To establish unmistakably, and clearly.

So, what is the purpose of writing?
1. To save a life.
2. To fix the holes.

—W. H.

ON EDUCATION, ART & WRITING

A Few Sticks of Dynamite to Wake You Up!

VARIOUS COLLECTED QUOTES BY EDWARD ABBEY:

"A formal education can sometimes be broadening but more often merely flattens."

"The best American writers have come from the hinterlands— Mark Twain, Theodor Dreiser, Jack London, Hemingway, Faulkner, Wolfe, Steinbeck. Most of them never went to college."

"The sneakiest form of literary subtlety, in a corrupt society, is to speak the plain truth. The critics will not understand you; the public will not believe you; your fellow writers will shake their heads. Laughter, praise, honors, money, and the love of beautiful girls will be your only reward."

"A critic is to an author as fungus is to an oak."

"Some people write to please, to soothe, to console. Others to provoke, to challenge, to exasperate and infuriate. I've always found the second approach to be more pleasing."

"Too many American authors have a servile streak where their backbone should be. Where's our latest Nobel laureate? More than likely you'll find him in the Rose Garden kissing the First Lady's foot."

"Great art is never perfect, perfect art is never great."

"Our suicidal poets (Plath, Berryman, Lowell, Jarrell, et al.) spent too much of their lives inside rooms and classrooms when they should have been trudging up mountains, slogging through swamps, rowing down rivers. The indoor life is the next best thing to premature burial."

"There is much to admire in the work of D. H. Lawrence—
   excepting his queer, gooey, and epicene prose."

"Most of what we call classic in world literature suggests artifacts
   in a wax museum. We have to hire and pay professors to get them read
   and talked about."

"It is not the writer's task to answer questions, but to question answers.
   To be impertinent, insolent, and, if necessary, subversive."

"Shakespeare wrote great poetry and prosperous plays.
   Who really cares…?"

"'Be fair,' say the temporizers,
   'tell both sides of the story.'
   But how do you be fair
   to both sides of a rape?
   Of a murder?
   Of a massacre?"

"Fence straddlers
   have no balls."

> *"Every great prince ought to be a great question asker."*
>
> — Machiavelli
> *The Prince*

ON TEACHING

G. B. S.

Recognize those initials? He was a critic of music, art, and drama. His writing for *The Saturday Review* made those initials famous; so famous, in fact, that George Bernard Shaw received the Nobel Prize for Literature in 1925.

G. B. S.

Teachers should know him well. He made one of the most maddening statements in all of history. This one statement, alone, *by itself*...has sent many teachers into a psychological bottomless pit.

They have cussed him.

They could kill him.

They hate him.

Sheesh! What on earth did he say?

Just this. (I quote)

> "People who know how to do anything go out and do it,
>   while those who do not know how to do anything
>   are obliged to earn a living by teaching."

Is it any wonder that he is called the greatest British satirist since Jonathan Swift? Great or not, he did use *satire* well. The intent of satire is to ridicule or censure. Why would he want to ridicule teachers?

I looked into it a little. I find it a paradox. He quit school at the age of fifteen . . . then went to work for five years in a land agent's office. When he was sixteen his mother left his alcoholic father; she went to London and *taught* music. When Shaw quit his land agent's office job, he went to "join" his mother. *His mother supported him for several years while he wrote five unsuccessful novels.*

In fact, he was not able to adequately support himself until another twenty-three years had passed. It was 1904 when Harley Granville-Barker "discovered" him and produced his plays at the Court Theatre. He had been married then for six years. He was forty-eight years old. It would be another twenty-one years to the Nobel Prize; then twenty-five more years 'til death struck him down. He was ninety-four.

What would he have had to do at twenty years of age if his mother had not supported his talent with the income from teaching music?

Did he hate his mother? Only God knows now.

BUT to be sure, a teacher today must be strong to survive the taunt of his classic remark. *Because he wasn't entirely wrong, you know!* About one-third of our teachers probably fall into that category. They are the ones we want to root out. They cause the stink.

The second one-third of all the teachers do not help, either. They are the ones who know how to play the game, brilliantly…but are not equipped to teach someone else how to play the game well. They are hired because of how they play their game, not because they know how to teach.

The last one-third is the reason most of us keep on keeping on. They are the ones who not only play brilliantly, but know how to reproduce that brilliance in others. *To those, we will take off our hats.*

I met my first one of *those* in the second grade. I'm not sure, but maybe G. B. S. never did meet one.

Too bad.

—W. H.

"GREAT TEACHERS DON'T TEACH."

"Socrates was one of the greatest teachers of all time, and all he did was walk around the streets and ask people irritating questions.

The great teacher makes a few simple points. The powerful teacher leaves one or two fundamental truths. And the memorable teacher makes the point not by telling, but by helping the students discover on their own.

All a really fine teacher does is make suggestions, point out problems, and above all, ask questions, and more questions, and more questions."

— JACOB NEUSNER
"Learning or learning how to think?"
The Fairfax Journal, September 3, 1991

"Teaching is far harder than doing. You will find a hundred who are brilliant football players for every one that can teach you to play the game well."

— W. W. Sawyer
Mathematician's Delight
1946

Joseph Mallord William Turner

He was elected to the Royal Academy at age twenty-seven, the youngest in history.

It was said of Turner that he was "fast and fluent." He bequeathed to the English government nineteen thousand drawings, three hundred oils, and three hundred watercolors. His studio contained, after his death, about twenty thousand more. It is estimated he sold and ruined another ten thousand. At his death he was in possession of about three million dollars (American equivalent) from the sale of his engravings of the English landscape.

He was, however, a poor teacher. The reason:

"Had trouble explaining what he wanted, too impatient to try."

— *The World of Turner*
Time/Life Series

ON "THE WALL"

"WHAT IS A DRAWING? How does one learn it? It is working through an invisible iron wall that seems to stand between what one *feels* and what one can *do*. How is one to get through that wall—since pounding against it is of no use? One must undermine the wall and drill through it slowly and patiently, in my opinion. And, look here, how can one continue such a work assiduously without being disturbed or distracted from it—unless one reflects and regulates one's life according to *principles?* And it is the same with other things as it is with art."

—VINCENT VAN GOGH

"PRINCIPLES"

WHAT *principles* do you suppose he had in mind? Without them, according to Van Gogh, there is no elimination of the "wall." The elimination of the wall requires "time" coupled with "assiduousness." Apparently the cost of learning to draw is too great to bear without the aid of "principles." And he said *that* same issue applies to all of life in general.

If we were to try to identify three principles…the knowing of which would motivate us to endure the grueling process of eliminating "the wall"…what would they be? I shall give you my ideas, please send me yours.

IDEA #1: *Principle:* **The prerequisite for the expression of your giftedness is the mastery of the basics.**

If you want to know the pleasure of painting, you must deal with drawing. Listen! Is it any wonder that the universal weakness of all artists of all time is drawing? Oh yes, make no mistake…if you can't draw, you can't paint. So if you have a gift in the area of painting…you will never know the "wonder" of it all if you don't draw.

And you will never draw with a "wall" in your way. So because of *that* principle, you are motivated to endure the war.

IDEA #2: *Principle:* **The higher you go, the thinner the air.**

One must understand that the closer you get to eliminating the wall, the fewer there are to identify with you. Most of the contestants will have settled for less. That's when true fellowship with those on the same altitude as you means so much. Rarer and rarer. Just like oxygen. The higher you go, the thinner the air.

The basic idea is this— as the battle goes on, you will need more and more air to breathe. You stop breathing and you stop working.

So there are two practical principles which emerge out of this second major idea:

1. Get time with men of like heart to keep you motivated. Do not compare yourself with your contemporaries but with the masters who have been where you want to go. Remember, to be a master you must be dead…and your works must survive your death.

2. Get plenty of air to breathe. I mean time alone. Time away. Time to think one more time about why you want to eliminate the wall. Time to commune with your Great Master.

IDEA #3: *Principle*: **Emotion is no substitute for action; action is no substitute for production.**

Do not fool yourself into thinking that because you are busy you are also productive. The mere fact that you are involved in a "siege" of the wall does not mean that it will fall. Action is not enough. Tears are not enough. There must also be wisdom involved. You need to be constantly on the alert and try every idea you can think of.

Remember *Troy?* The Greeks pulled off the longest siege I know about…it lasted 10 years, and ended about 1194 B.C. *But* they were only productive *when* they struck upon a novel idea. You know the rest.

But emotion and violent activity were *not enough* to knock the wall down for the Germans at **Verdun** in 1916. Their siege against the French lasted 298 days…then they gave up.

     Nor was emotion and activity *enough* for the Germans at **Leningrad.**
       The siege lasted 28 months.
     Nor was emotion and activity *enough* for the Germans at **Stalingrad.**
       The siege endured for 166 days.
     Nor was emotion and activity *enough* for the North Vietnamese at **Khe Sanh, Vietnam.** The siege lasted 76 days.

Remember, victory does *not come* for the emotional person. Victory does *not come* for the active person. There is *no* substitute for production.

*T*HREE *Principles.* I wonder if Van Gogh had these in mind:
  1. The prerequisite for the expression of a gift is the mastery of the basics.
  2. The higher you go, the thinner the air.
  3. Emotion is no substitute for action. Action is no substitute for production.

For your benefit, go back and read the quote by Van Gogh at the beginning of this letter; then read the following definition of *assiduousness:*

    "careful and unremitting application."

REMEMBER, **"…pounding against it is of no use."**

— W. H.

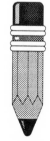

"Do it again and again, ten times, a hundred times."

— **D**EGAS

" NEVER alter a drawing. Never use an eraser. Throw it away if it goes
   wrong, and begin again. And remember, sketching is what roosters do
   as they scratch in the dirt looking for a meal of their own *manure*.
   You are supposed to be learning to draw."

" THE *difference* between sketching and drawing is this:
   all sketching is preparatory— all drawing is final.
   There is no need for preparatory sketching if one knows how to draw.
   Abandon, therefore, sketching for the rest of your life."

" ERASERS. Are they not the curse of the art student?
   Make up your mind to *never* use an eraser to do anything other than
   remove smudges that are left by something other than drawing...
   like dirty hand prints or smearing caused by mishandling of a surface.
   If drawing is always final, why do you need an eraser?"

— W. H.

"HE was drawing on a copper plate in the Louvre...
   before 'Infantes' by Velasquez, when he first made acquaintance with Manet.
   The slightly older painter, already the talk of Paris, stopped before Degas
   in astonishment, 'You're not afraid ?' he asked. 'I should never dare
   engrave like that without a preliminary sketch.'
   Degas only smiled."

"FORAIN, an artist who was a friend of Degas, said at his funeral,
   'He greatly loved drawing. So do I.'"

— From the life of Edgar Degas
Time/Life Series

QUESTION:

Are you afraid to come out from behind your mask ?

"WHY not
go out on a limb?
Isn't that
where the fruit is?"
— FRANK SCULLY

"WHY not
upset the apple cart?
If you don't,
the apples will rot anyway."
— FRANK A. CLARK

"Oh,
the girl who used to be me—
she could fly;
she was free;
and she wrote all the words to have fun.
Yes, the girl who used to be me, used to go dancing;
And I feel she's been gone too long.
I'd like the chance to be the girl who used to be me."
— from the movie *Shirley Valentine*

"The soul is constantly about to starve;
it cannot live on fun alone.
If the soul gets no other food,
it will first tear apart other creatures
...then itself."

— Selma Lagerlöf
Introduction
Letters from the Country
by Carol Bly

❖

"Where there is no private life
there is no enthusiasm,
and there is little enough
enthusiasm in our towns....
People are taught to be drones."

— Carol Bly
Letters from the Country

"**I** had managed to meet every challenge
thrown at me professionally. In fact,
I succeeded beyond my wildest dreams.
But it felt empty.
I was losing my soul, and
I didn't even realize it."

— PEG WATKINS
Sky Magazine of Delta Airlines
March 1993

"*IF you want
to
win
anything
— a race, your self,
your life—
you have to go
a
little
berserk.*"

— GEORGE SHEEHAN
Quoted in *Do It! Let's Get Off Our Buts*
by John Roger and Peter McWilliams

❖

"*UTTERING a new word, or taking a new step, is what people fear the most.*"

— FYODOR DOSTOEVSKY

MODEL DEFINITELY NOT FOUND
AT THE KENNY PENNY
RESTAURANT IN
FABENS, TEXAS...

AMERICAN WOMEN?

"Who will set them free to be people, too?
Society is not their enemy. They themselves are.
They must live or die based upon the fire in their soul just like I do.
My job, as a teacher, is to tell them that."

— W. H.

ON A DANGEROUS COMPOSITION

I aimed at a painting yesterday, and hit it. But I do believe it is the most dangerous composition I have ever attempted. It works, but only by the skin of my teeth.

Have you ever broken every rule you ever knew, and still come out smelling like a rose? It is not like I did all this bad arrangement on purpose, but when it was all said and done it had definitely "happened" to me. It was a strange combination of "v's" that all ended up pointing to an area a couple of inches below "the idiot line." The weird composition does move the eye around, and may even be a stroke of genius. All of that will become obvious, or not obvious, when the work is framed, photographed or on the wall.

But for sure, today's work will be different. It is possible that I painted beyond myself…but my good sense (I hope it is good) tells me I need to "come home" for the next one.

WHAT does coming home mean to me?

Five things:

THING ONE: Warmer, with yellows, oranges, raw siennas, light pinks, blues. Not so wild. More sky.

THING TWO: Let nature feed me a little. Don't revolt against what you see so violently. There was a beauty there you admired when you photographed it. Keep that in mind.

THING THREE: Remember grace and beauty of style. Approach it more gently.

THING FOUR: Keep it managed in such a way as to have more simple areas to hug and kiss the complicated ones.

THING FIVE: It is said that the way a painter uses grays is an indication of his skill and understanding. I need to remember that.

HOPELESSLY in love with it all,

— W. H.

"DON'T be the one who knows how to do it, but the one who recognizes beauty when it comes…then stops.
Add to your work that quality of looking accidental.
You may not know what you want,
but you should know what you don't want.
When you get it, be intelligent enough to stop."

— CHARLES WEBSTER HAWTHORNE
Taken from the Newsletter of the
Niagra Frontier Watercolor Society, June 12, 1991

QUESTION:

———

Are you a "know it all"?

"**S**TUDENTS usually come at the painting process wanting to know it all, and wanting an immediate and detailed explanation during a demonstration. To illustrate how hard this is, think of a great and important part of mathematics: the square root of minus one— something which no one has ever seen or felt or tasted. Yet there is no doubt about its properties. I feel the same way about telling a student to paint not individual objects, but rather their relationship. I know how to do it, and there is no mistaking the joy of seeing it work. Yet, how do you see, feel or taste the "relationship" of one form to another?"

— W. H.

ON PUTTING
FIRST THINGS FIRST

TODAY I was severely tempted to take off three days to take care of business. That would be a great mistake.

Three reasons:

ONE: **I must stay in my pace.** If a runner breaks pace it is quite serious. It puts the whole race in jeopardy. It also interrupts the joy, and the peace. So, then, I will take care of business this afternoon. Before that, I will not.

TWO: **My juices are rolling.** To write, to draw, to paint is in my heart. I cannot learn if I do them in fits and starts. No more of that.

THREE: **I can do more than I think in less time than I think.** To spend time anxious over that which is only trivial is worse than a tragedy. I cannot afford to be tyrannized by the urgent.

> **K**EEP important things important.
> The long haul is what matters.
>
> — W. H.

"THAT DAD GUM OWNER
OF MINE IS GOING TO
WAIT TILL MORNING TO
FEED ME ONE
MORE TIME!"

*"**I**F you pick up a starving dog and make him prosperous,
he will not bite you.
This is the principle difference
between a man and his dog."*

— MARK TWAIN

"IF *you can't bark with the big dogs, don't sit on the front porch.*"

— MARIO FERRANTE
Artist and High School Art Teacher
Auburn, California

BARKING LIKE REMBRANDT

How does one get to the "front porch"?

In other words, what makes an artist think on the level of great work? How can someone keep from being just another painter that lived, died, and inspired no great admiration? If I could narrow the key factors down to three, what would they be?

ONE: *You must have a heart.* I mean a heart for the task. The task is to be completely novel, unique, totally you . . . and the maker of a great gift for the benefit of others, and to the praise of the author of your life. Those without a "heart" will *never drink in the challenge.* They cannot, indeed, comprehend the task. To say it differently, a person will not set out for a city he knows nothing about. Listen to this piece of advice given sixty years after the death of Christ:

> "First say to yourself what you would be,
>   and then *do what you have to do."*
>   — EPICTÉTUS

To put it plainly, you must have a heart for the heat. If you don't, the fire will scare you away.

TWO: *You must have some insight.* Those who do what other people don't are the really creative ones out there. To do that, you must be *looking at* painting from a totally original point of view — a new or *unique sight into the game.* It was Emerson who made the observation that genius is simply a matter of *seeing what other people don't.* What slice of the pie do you want to eat? Where is the target you want to hit? What is your special insight?

THREE: *You must have perspective.* This is the rare one. Most living artists do not have a healthy perspective on their talent. To have perspective one must keep the long view in mind as they handle short range activities. *The greatest indication of a bad perspective is this: You have been sucked into competing with your contemporaries.* Hey!

It is a disease.

An ego trip.

A way to waste all your energy.

What is it?

Trying to outpace your friend.

If you are not attempting to bark like Rembrandt, then just stop.

—W. H.

*"If a man who paints only the tree, or flower,
or other surface he sees before him,
were an artist,
the king of artists would be the photographer."*

— James McNeil Whistler
The Gentle Art of Making Enemies

"…I have been at work all day;
what a happy life. What a divine
compensation for my isolated state
as they call it!…
I hasten to this enchanting work
as to the feet of the most
cherished mistress."

— Eugene Delacroix
writing to Madame de Forget
Age 62, 1852

"People who start up companies
are like painters or writers;
often so caught up in a project that
they don't go home for days at a time,
sometimes forgetting to eat
until food is brought to them."

— "Land of Plenty: In the Silicon Valley,
Hot Ideas Mix with Venture Cash"
Wall Street Journal, August 2, 1983

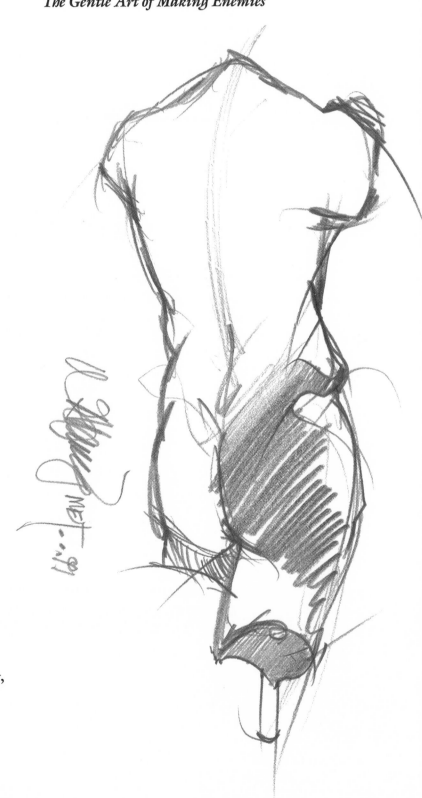

"Finishing
a painting
demands
a
heart
of
steel."

— Eugene Delacroix

"...good health,
good looks,
good intellect,
abundant energy,
a well-balanced temperament
and, added to all this,
a clear head for business."

A description of Peter Paul Rubens
— C. V. Wedgewood
and editors of Time/Life Books

"His principle quality, if one may be preferred among so many,
is a prodigious spirit, that is to say, a prodigious life;
without it, no artist is really great...
Titian and Paul Veronese are tame beside him."

— Eugene Delacroix
speaking of Rubens

QUESTION:

Do you have guts?

"THERE came a day when the mentor
told Bronfman, the young pianist,
that it was time to 'sink or swim.'
Bronfman looked him in the eye,
and said,
'Take me to the lake!'"

— SOURCE UNKNOWN

"IN his last year at West Point, and a few weeks before his marriage,
Patton suddenly stood up and stuck his head into the line of fire
during some sharpshooting exercises.

LATER, when asked by his Dad why, he replied, 'I just wanted to see
how afraid I'd be, and train myself not to be scared.'"

— GENERAL GEORGE PATTON
from *Patton: Ordeal and Triumph*
by Ladislas Farago

"I**T** is not vocabulary
that one seeks in a writer,
but
verve
guts
smash
romance
flair
and the touch of fantasy.

It is not facts but feelings
that propel a writer.

It is the same with a painter."

— W. H.

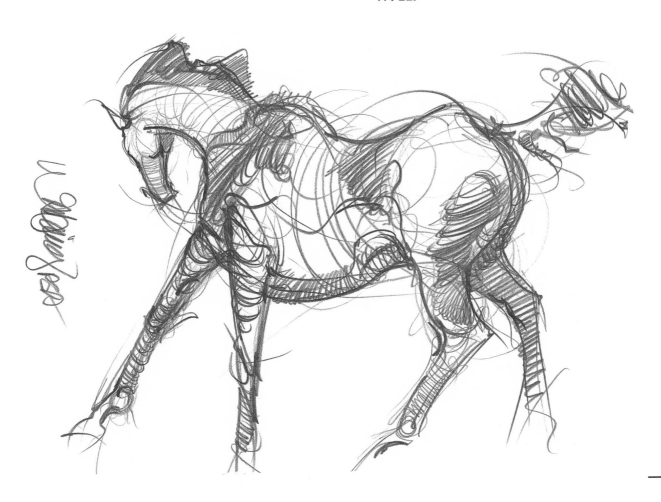

ON BEING STRONG

"GIVE me the young man who
has brains enough to make a fool of himself."

— ROBERT LOUIS STEVENSON
Crabbed Age and Youth

"YOU cannot run away from weakness;
you must sometime fight it out or perish;
and if that be so, why not now, and where you stand?"

— ROBERT LOUIS STEVENSON
The Amateur Emigrant

"INDIVIDUALITY is the salt of common life.
You may have to live in a crowd,
but you do not have to live like it, nor subsist on its food."

— YOUNG EWING ALLISON
The School of Life

"YOU don't learn to hold your own in this world
by standing on guard, but by attacking,
and getting well hammered yourself."

— GEORGE BERNARD SHAW
Getting Married

A TASTE FOR FIRE

THIS was his moment:
Major General
Commander: Western Task Force
Forced Landing French Morocco
33845 Americans
29 transports
4 days from his 57th birthday
33rd year in the Army
14 knots

"It seems that my whole life has been pointed to this moment"

Then the General wrote at the bottom of his journal: "I can't decide logically if I am a man of destiny or a lucky fool, but I think I am destined. Five more days will show."

And they did.

NAME: George S. Patton

He had a unique place in history.

And so is the make-up of *every lump of clay.*

Do you believe that your whole life is pointed somewhere? Is it by careless pointlessness that you have a desire to be a painter?

LET's get some fellowship of mind with one of the "greats" in history. Let him talk to you *about inspiration*. . about that horizon of sunlight in which you long to stroll. Let's ask him to tell us the difference between an *old painter* and an *old master.*

Mr. Joseph M.W. Turner, Esq., R.A., please open your inner vault...and tell us how to be great!

I will tell you how greatness in art was— and was not— achieved. Not patrons, influential relatives, nor even perseverance and industry could push an artist to the 'heights.' The key, rather, was an *innate power* that enforces, that inspires, and without which labor would be...a vain drudgery.

An "innate power."

What did his *contemporaries* think of *his* work? Here is a brief picture of their attitudes:

...he painted whatever and however he chose. Other artists...found his unpredictability maddening. No sooner had they decided that Turner had settled down than he would stun them with some fresh outrage...

…bewildering versatility…

Crudities of execution, excesses of color and unseemly revelations of the painter's psyche.

A Turner painting never looked quite finished. The forms were not at all well defined, and whole sections of the picture were indistinct; one had to work at figuring out his intent…Turner's paint almost lunged out at the viewer instead of being smoothly finished as academic tradition dictated: he seemed to have laid it on with a kind of brutal relish, then further hacked it up with a palette knife…colors arbitrarily chosen…applied in blobs and dabs…bright…defying the customary dark tones.....

…a diseased eye and a reckless hand…

Good grief!

I hope it is obvious to you that you cannot depend upon other people to determine your value. Some of you out there have that same class of giftedness (the diseased eye and reckless hand). **The world really does wait for you.**

Now is a good time to make your move.

Allow me to end this letter with a few thoughts from General Patton with regard to how you might consider handling the decisions lying in front of you:

Listen!

Those who grab their opportunities, however hazardous they appear to be, have a distinct advantage over others limited by their narrow view of the vistas that lay beyond. I have encountered timidity under many other names— patience, moderation, reasonability, or logic— all my life…I am not congenitally opposed to reason, but I am dead set against letting it ruin a good chance.

May the chances you take
lead you to *your* moment of greatness.

— W. H.

————

P.S. By the way, Turner did have some people who appreciated him. For example, John Ruskin, the "supreme arbiter of English art," said of Turner: "He has been sent as a prophet of God to reveal to men the mysteries of His universe."
(If it is not one extreme, it's the other!)

" Bradley will lead the invasion. But he is just a limited-objective general. When we get moving, Patton is the man with the drive and imagination to do the dangerous things fast."
— General George C. Marshall, July 27, 1944
from *Patton: Ordeal and Triumph*
by Ladislos Farago

Hᴇ resolved to condition himself against fear,
and set a course of training that seemed as reckless and foolish to the outsider
as it was purposeful and systematic to him. During his equestrian exercises and contests,
he regularly sought out the most difficult obstacles and the highest hurdles,
not to show off— as was actually believed by his audiences—
but as part of his training to overcome his fears.

— Describing General George Patton
    from *Patton: Ordeal and Triumph*
    by Ladislos Farago

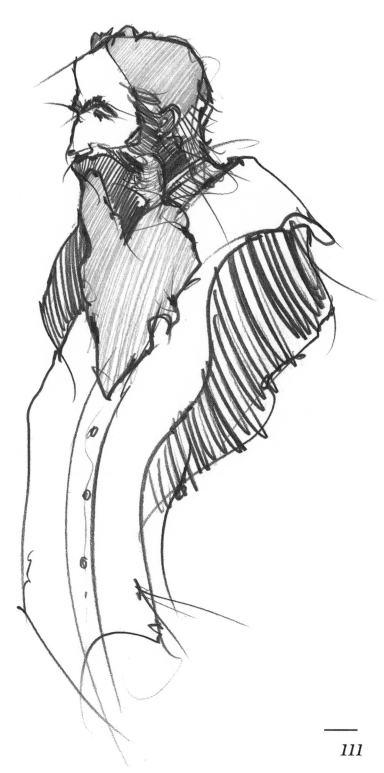

"Iᴛ joined up in sheer impulse
and ended up in the trenches in Flanders.
Whatever you mean by hell on earth,
that was the trenches.

And yet I relished it.
Can you understand that?
I lived more, felt more, in one day
than in a year of ordinary living.
Life became real, exciting.
I couldn't get enough.

That, to me,
was the 'real world.'"

        — Jᴀᴄᴋ Hɪɢɢɪɴs
            Night of the Fox

*"**I**f you want to launch big ships,*
you have to go
where the water is deep."

— Conrad Hilton

TO THOSE WHO HAVE
TROUBLE WITH THE PAST

Last year I was spending a June summer in the mountains of Cloudcroft, New Mexico. While there, I happened upon a book which strangely affected my mind. It was the autobiography of **Conrad Hilton**: *Be My Guest.*

It was key to my life then. I was contemplating incredible changes in my life. I was plagued morosely by self-doubt and fear. It was *my past* that was eating my lunch. For some reason, my emotional attachments to the mediocre performances of my past seemed to bind me in terms of being different. It was almost as if I would be dishonest and a fake if I set out to be what I knew I was not. Know what I mean?

Now **Hilton** was something else! And he was from my part of the country. And he even built his second hotel in El Paso, Texas. That's my home. I was interested. He was a businessman, and an idealist…and he combined *both* in an amazing lifestyle surrounding the creation of the world's first international hotel network. From his point of view, "If business didn't cross frontiers, armies would." He saw his life in terms of destiny. He had a supremely honorable sense of value and worth…and *believed* one man…*any nobody…could* make a permanent difference.

As an idealist, he made a few classic statements that show how he felt. Here are a few examples:

1. *He was oriented toward fixing things*…he used to quote another saying: "It is better to light one candle than to curse the darkness."

2. *He had a dream that burned in his mind*: "An integral part of my dream was to show the countries most exposed to Communism the other side of the coin— the fruits of the free world."

3. *He saw Communism as an enemy to the worth of every individual:* "The essence of Communism is the death of the individual and the burial of his remains in a collective mess."

4. Yet *he was international in his thinking,* and believed that his business of building hotels in other countries would contribute to real solutions among people. He used to

refer to a quote from Byzantium in 658 B.C. (also known as Constantinople and Istanbul, Turkey) which reflected a real bottom line custom among their people: "After you drink a cup of coffee with me, that commits you to friendship for 40 years."

5. *Born into time as a child of unique pressures, he felt the load, and often prayed:* "Be swift to save us, dear God, before the darkness falls."

WHAT is *your* dream? Are you short on idealism? Are you convinced that you can make a difference? Are you struggling with a "breaking away" from your past?

Remember this: you are unique and very special. Learn from your past and step out to be what you ought to be. Then you will make a difference.

Why?

Because of what **Will Rogers** said:

"People's minds are changed by *observation*, not argument."

WHEN they see, they will follow without a word.
Hilton helped do that for me.

— W. H.

"WHATEVER you do, you need courage.
Whatever course you decide upon,
there is always someone
to tell you you are wrong.
There are always difficulties arising
which tempt you to believe
your adversaries are right."

— EMERSON

"DON'T take your own history so seriously.
Stonewall Jackson's lowest marks at West Point were in infantry tactics,
a field in which he made a world-wide reputation."

— CHESTY PULLER
Marine

What I Am Like

I am a bee,

everyday I search for something new.

I am a door,

everytime I open I find something new.

I am a flower,

I produce a fragrant aroma.

I am a lamp,

when I light up I help somebody.

I am a paintbrush,

I give color to my family's life.

I am a piece of plastic,

no matter what I cover you can always see who I am.

I am a blanket,

I give warmth and comfort to anybody who needs it.

I am a tree,

I bend with the wind.

I am a carrousel horse,

I am jewel studded by the grace of GOD.

I am a piece of wood,

shaped by the Carpenter's hand.

— Carolyn Charlese Herring
Poem for Honors English
Age 12, March 15, 1992
Clint, Texas

> *"A man is likely to mind his own business
> when it is worth minding.
> When it is not, he takes his mind off
> his own meaningless affairs
> by minding other people's business."*
>
> — ERIC HOFFER
> *The True Believer*

ON MANAGING PEOPLE

NOTHING is more valuable than an *individual person.*
Not money
Not success
Not power
Not prestige
Not fame
Not greatness

If that is true, and you have several of them around you...how do you make them do what you want? How do you make them serve your interests? How can you guarantee they will do what matters to you?

ANSWER: *You don't.*

PEOPLE are so important that they need to be served...not managed. You have heard it before, you must do for them what you would want them to do for you.

That may include believing in them as you would want to be believed in. It may be asking them to do something they never thought they could do. It might even require that you ask them to join a team so that they might learn the power of synergy . . . thereby liberating them from a lifestyle centered around themselves. In fact, you might even ask them to do the very thing you do.

That is, of course, the greatest thing you can do for anyone: Be what you want them to be. An example...an inspiring one, is the rarest thing I have ever encountered. And, those encounters have changed my life.

So how do you really manage people? By serving their best interests. I have never found any effort too hard when I follow that concept.

By the way, what is the opposite of serving people?

ANSWER: *Using them.*

DON'T ever do that.

—W. H.

A student once asked Whistler:
"Why are you a painter?"
Whistler answered quickly:
"Because an artist
has to do SOMETHING!"

"WHAT'S UP, DOC?"

WHEN you get to my age, you have been asked "How are you?"
about five million times.

IT takes other forms, like these:
What's happening in your life?
What's been going on?
What's cookin'?
What's up?

So for years I've been working on some answers.

It bothers me so much because I fight boredom so much. Anything that trivializes life, that makes it sound dull or regular or colorless, *that* makes me uneasy. Life is hard enough.

Consequently, just to inject life into the circle of my own sight, I search for ways to transform my existence.

So, therefore, so, so, so, I have come up with an answer. It is as if I "play like" those who ask me the question do it for me, not them. I just imagine that God pulls people out of his pockets to jump-start my mornings. After all, I can't hear my answer if I am not asked the question.

And the answer sounds so neat. The twist and curve of the words are like honey after a meal of tacos or enchiladas. The words do for me what *The Sound of Music* does to my family. The answer is like a sunset. It is like reading the writings of my Daddy.

I laugh.

I jiggle.

I wiggle.

It is an answer that is something cooked up just to entice the taste buds of a starving man, namely me.

QUESTION: "So, what's up, Doc?"
ANSWER: *"I am all caught up in the full play of my own existence."*

—W. H.

"A
*genius
is always on duty,
even his thoughts are
tax deductible."*

—EDWARD ABBEY

*"**N**EVER retreat.*
Never explain.
Get it done.
Let them howl."

— BENJAMIN JOWETT

TO THOSE
WHO LOVE COLOR

EVER had someone's jealous criticism eat into your soul? Ever take bold color risks, only to hear some small soul *spit venom in your ear*?

You know, most people think on the level of a zoo-bound sloth. Anything that threatens the security of their leisurely ignorance deserves an attack. (If something is "different" it is "wrong.")

There is such a big deal going around for the look of reality. If the color you use isn't real, then bite, bite, bite. It is as if they never heard of Monet, or Gaugin, or Van Gogh, or Delacroix, or Turner. Turning haystacks blue is no new thing.

Or Orange.

Or Violet.

Or Wild Pink.

Or Pouncing Passionate Red.

Besides, if you use drawing, the form created by the line of the drawing defines the motif. You are then *really* loosened for the use of abstract color. I still believe that the world has yet to see what gifted artists can do with ideas that were introduced by such inept painters as Matisse and Cezanne.

WHAT could a *new artist* who has kissed heaven
do with the *old idea* of fauvism?

—W. H.

118

*"*Gray *is the enemy of all painting…banish therefore all dull colors.*"

— Eugene Delacroix
The World of Delacroix
by Tom Prideaux
and editors of Time/Life Books

"Pianist Vladimir Horowitz asked the advice
of the great conductor Arturo Toscanini.
'If you want to please the critics,' Toscanini told him,
'don't play too loud, too soft, too fast, too slow.'"

— Quoted from *Do It! Lets Get Off Our Buts*
by John Roger and Peter McWilliams

A FUNDAMENTAL TRUTH

ONE might ask, shouldn't a student wanting to make a living as an artist go to an art school? You would think it would be logical. Asking a similar question— should a budding entrepreneur study entrepreneuring at a school by the same name? The answer is: "Sure, *if* there were any true entrepreneurs teaching there! But, such a school must not be built around professors who study people who are entrepreneurs. Real entrepreneurs ought to teach entrepreneuring."

There is a fundamental truth here. Entrepreneurs breed entrepreneurs, but *professors breed professors*. In thinking about art, consider this: *where are the art professors who are making a living by selling the art they create?* Will not the professor multiply people just like himself, who must teach to make a living? Would such a teacher tell a new student that he, the student, can make a living in art if the teacher both *never did* and *never learned how*? If the teacher was asked by the student whether a living could be made, and the teacher said yes, then the student would ask the teacher why he wasn't doing it. The answer to that question would be *very painful*. That is, of course, why the professor would never tell the student that the student could indeed do what the teacher never did.

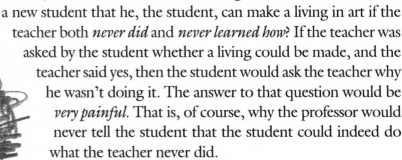

THUS, my philosophy.

I encourage an art student to study the principles that will enable him to succeed, such as *marketing*. He should study art with a real artist in *private*. Meanwhile, this student in marketing class has it one up on the other marketing students because he is learning in the context of reality: namely, he himself is what he is marketing. So the university, then, becomes his development time for the enabling of his gift (art) in the marketplace. What student in marketing already has something real to market?

Mine would.

THUS, the genius of this approach.

—W. H.

"The true character of the student is one of great mental and spiritual activity.
He arrives at conclusions and he searches to express his findings.
He goes to the market place, to the exhibition place,
wherever he can reach the people, to lay before them his new angle on life.
He creates a disturbance, wins attention from those who have in them
his kind of blood— the student blood. These are stirred into activity.
Camps are established. Discussion runs high. There is life in the air.

The non-student element says it is heresy.
Let us have 'peace!' Put the disturber in jail."

—Robert Henri
The Art Spirit

❖

*"We are not called to make a revolution
but to lead a revolutionary life."*

—C. Rene Padilla
Latin American Theological Fraternity Bulletin
1977, No.2

"From my observation of men and boys
I am inclined to think that my way of study
is the common way, the natural way,
and that the schoolmasters destroy it
and replace it by something
that conduces to mere learning."

—John Perry
1901

❖

*"If you would paint every day for seven months
you wouldn't need a teacher."*

—Robert Henri
The Art Spirit

*"If what you want to sell
doesn't sell,
you are not truly being creative."*

— JAY CONRAD LEVINSON
Guerilla Marketing

ON THE IMPRINT
OF YOUR LIPSTICK

In the last year of her life, a twelve year old girl modeled for Sir Thomas Lawrence. He called his painting of her "Pinkie."

This work of art was bought in 1926 by the master art dealer, Duveen. He purchased it for $375,000 at Christies in London. It was then offered to Andrew Mellon, the Secretary of the Treasury of the United States, who said that the price Duveen wanted was "outrageous."

While Duveen admitted that the price he wanted was "steep," he repeated to Mellon what was one of his cardinal truths: "When you pay high for the priceless, you're getting it cheap." Mellon still turned it down. But, H. E. Huntington didn't. Today it hangs in the Huntington Museum near Pasadena.

My advice to the artist:

Great art is priceless. It is the face of our civilization, the signature of our culture. Do not think for a moment you should not ask a high price for what you do. Whatever they pay is too little. People can go around buying thousand dollar works all they want. But, how often do they have the chance to buy one for five thousand? Or thirty? Or sixty? Or half a million? You offer them a *bite* of history, and a chance to *dine* at the table of our culture. *Never* let someone who rejects one of your works look down on you as if you were trying to get to them by some slick casting of a plastic covered trash object into their lap. You are, unlike all the other professions, in the business of **kissing the joy as it flies by,** and then **offering them the imprint of your lipstick.** It will be an adornment for the inner world of their emotions, those emotions that are cultivated within the private walls of the residence in which they dwell. *You allow them to touch the joy of life.* You, the artist, will be for them what is described by the writer Edward Abbey:

"What is the job of the artist? To be a miracle worker. To make the blind see, the dull feel, the dead to live."

The kisses you offer are priceless, and whatever they pay is cheap.

"He who binds to himself a joy
   Does the winged life destroy;
   But he who kisses the joy as it flies
   Lives in Eternity's sun rise."

— WILLIAM BLAKE

THEREFORE, make up your mind to *kiss* the joy as it flies by, and then
sell the imprint of your lipstick to the one for which it was made.

—W. H.

———————

P.S. As a man I sometimes find it hard to identify with lipstick planted on a flying parcel
of joy. But it helps to know, as I heard it said by a Native American Indian, that *"I am
half woman on my mother's side."*

"YOU are the organization.
   You answer to yourself
   You make the rules and break the rules.
   And that means you get to be
            amazing
                    outrageous
                            surprising
                                    unpredictable
                                            brilliant,
                                                    and quick.
   But don't delude yourself into believing that you can
   suceed with no advertising."

— JAY CONRAD LEVINSON
Guerilla Marketing

IT is not possible to sell everything to everybody, nor is it necessary.
If you try to sell everything to everybody, you'll end up selling
everything to nobody or nothing to everybody.
Instead you should strive to sell something to somebody.

Your art is the "something."
Your buyer is the "somebody."

Adapted from thoughts of
— JAY CONRAD LEVINSON
Guerilla Marketing

SLEEPING WITH CADAVERS

*WHAT must an artist remember
if he is to keep the "smell of life" in his work?*

THREE things to keep in mind, adapted from the thoughts of writer Edward Abbey:
  1. PRINCIPLE: *Inspiration is more important than technique* because technique should be invented after you get a visual pulse of hot motivation. Abbey said it in this manner: "In art as in a boat, a bullet, or a coconut-cream pie, purpose determines form." How and what and if you *see* is what matters, then invent.

  2. PRINCIPLE: *Your method can force you out of your own mold* into something foreign to who you are as an artist. Consider this thought: "The writer more concerned with technique than truth becomes a technician, not an artist." I am sick to death of technical wizardry displayed in the arena of national art competitions. A work should always be more artistic than technical to get my vote.

  3. PRINCIPLE: *Perspiration is of no value if it does not function out of a well-spring of inspiration.* Abbey said this: "Good writing may be defined as having something to say and saying it well. When one has nothing to say, one should remain silent. Silence is always beautiful at such times."

  Dionysius the Elder said: "Let your speech be better than silence, or be silent."

ALL of these principles speak to the idea that imagination is the key to keeping yourself alive as an artist.

  Three principles said in a different way:

    PRINCIPLE ONE: Your visual idea should determine technical method.

    PRINCIPLE TWO: A technician is not an artist, just a slave to a look.

    PRINCIPLE THREE: A habit of perspiration is of no value without a habit of inspiration.

        WRITERS and artists face some of the same pitfalls.
        Stay out of them!

                       — W. H.

P.S. All I want to say can be hammered into one little quote —

      "JANE AUSTEN: *Getting into her books
      is like getting into bed with a cadaver.
      Something vital is lacking; namely, life."*

                     — EDWARD ABBEY

ENOUGH IS ENOUGH

ALEXANDER Archipenko, a sculptor from the Russian Ukraine, enjoyed quite a reputation in the United States in the 1920's. He was known for his cubistic creations, and especially for his "creative" use of negative space...or "voids."

I regard him highly, however, only for one of his quotes. While living in Hollywood, in the 1930's, he said this to some of his friends: he was

"doing pioneer work and educating the ignorant."

Having been in the dairy business for many years, I came to understand the meaning of "pioneer work and educating the ignorant." I was pioneering in the art of doing embryo transplants in a commercial dairy herd environment, for the purpose of advancing the genetics of milk production, only. I did, along with my team, seventy-six embryo transplants personally...and know the terrible impact of trying to 'pioneer' in the face of 'ignorance' on the part of those who set policy.

However, pioneering in the art world is far different than pioneering in the dairy business. Most "pioneering" is simply an ego in pursuit of a new art form. To be frank, it is not from ignorance that such "prophets of novelty" are opposed. When they magnify their digression away from absolutes, then call it progress...and further, call me ignorant because of my commensurate disgust.... *That's* when I issue a public cry for a high tech depository mechanism that would allow the presentation of a couple of tons of old-time dairy manure on their door-step.

*E*NOUGH *is enough.*

— W. H.

P.S. It is not the inventor of a new kind of pencil that deserves praise, but the one who knows how to use the regular pencil with the grace of an angel.

QUESTION:
What is the finest statement ever made about modern art?

ANSWER: *"A product of the untalented, sold by the unprincipled, to the utterly bewildered."*

— AL CAPP

ON FREE-THINKING

I have nothing against it.
If it stays in bounds!
How can someone feel free to think without restriction,
and yet stay in "bounds?"

To illustrate, I think it is a lot like sex.

Sex is great.
Sex is good.
Dear God, I wish everyone would!

Indeed— but *in marriage, not out.* When you think
outside of this range, then you get to play
with fun things like syphllis.

THE same goes for art.
Art is great.
Art is good.

But for *Art News* to publish a painting
of a nude male standing in a gigantic bowl
while masturbating is a bit much.

Such freedom ought to be suppressed.

(Actually, some of these people provide
a good argument for those who are
in favor of abortion.)

—W. H.

> *"God is really only another artist.*
> *He invented the giraffe, the elephant, the ant.*
> *He has no real style.*
> *He just goes on trying other things."*
>
> — Pablo Picasso

ON HORSE RACING

At fifty-three, fifty-seven, or some unbelievable age, Willy Shoemaker has just won another one. Can you believe it?

I mean, this horse racing thing is a big deal. Just this last summer the Ruidoso racetrack sank another million into improvements. At Sunland Park officials recently said they were depressed because people were only betting $343,000 a day. In the Jockey Club, it will cost you between $60,000 and $100,000 just to own a seat on the finish line. People (the ladies) come up to the Jockey Club dressed like queens. *It was there that I saw, for the first time, diamonds crawling up the sides of ears.* Diamonds on glasses. A friend of mine even stopped me one time to do a quick drawing of the Treasurer of the United States.

Movie stars,
Governors,
Big whigs,
Even little whigs.

Even saw Mr. T. for Pete's sake.
I even met a guy named Pete.

ALL this leads me to say that *there really must be something about horses.* Ever see such a to-do over frogs or mosquitoes?

BETTER learn to paint the horse.
You won't be sorry.

— W. H.

HORSE @ LAS COLINAS

W Wagner '91

"*Titian* would have been a great painter
— if he had drawn better."

— Michelangelo

"A DOG,
the only thing on this earth
that loves you
more than he loves himself."

— JOSH BILLINGS

IN HONOR
OF MY DOG,
PETE.

I love you, Buddy!

—W. H.

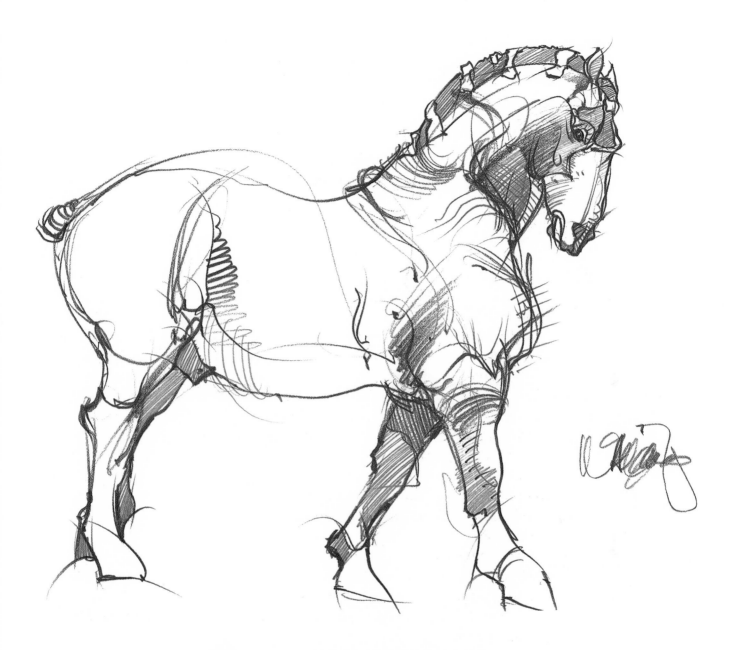

> *"WHAT is real is not the external form but the essence of things."*
>
> — CONSTANTIN BRANCUSI
> **Sculptor**
> **1876 - 1957**

> *"NO great artist ever sees things as they really are. If he did, he would cease to be an artist."*
>
> — OSCAR WILDE

ROBIN HOOD, LADY MARIAN & CLINT, TEXAS:

It is a Monday, 9:30 in the morning at the coffee shop in Clint, Texas.

Do you not marvel at the fact that this letter makes its way to you? You know, there are a million places to live. Why am I located only a long flight of a pheasant from the Mexican border? Why do I write to you? Not a soul here has even the foggiest notion about what I do. Such are the twists of life in a country where we all do exactly as we wish in the context of the freedom we enjoy under law. Each man enjoys his own universe.

My soul was stirred by watching the movie, *Robin Hood, Prince of Thieves* last afternoon. Is not this fiction more true to real life than so much of life is? Is not that which is imaginary more of a key than the ones we carry in our pocket? For example, Robin Hood tells Lady Marian that he has learned much by war. Although of "noble" birth himself, he tells her that his time in the crusades changed how he thinks. He said, actually quoting his father, "Nobility is not a birth right." He said he was profoundly affected when he saw "a lowly peasant pull a sword out of his own chest to defend a dying horse."

Later, Lady Marian will do for love of Robin Hood what she would not do for the King. Love and devotion and honor and pride (a pride of honest character and integrity) transform the ruffians of Sherwood Forest.

How neat.

How wonderful.

How grand.

And as a trump card, the movie shows us well that there are surprises waiting for us that will totally alter our perception of things: such as, when Christian tells Robin he is his half brother.

Above all I see this, that *heart counts.*

Courage counts.

Your voice counts.

Your presence counts.

One man against all wrong may not prevail, but maybe he will. But surely one will never know if he does not put his life on the line.

His heart. His life. His blood.

I only have one chance to die well.

But if I live to seventy I will have about 9,409 chances to live well. As Robin Hood. As his Moorish friend. As his blind companion.

Clearly, if you have nothing to die for, you will be at a total loss with regard to what you live for.

WHAT are you living for, man?

Maybe you should do yourself the honor of treating your wretched heart with a color bound experience of hope and love and courage found in the recent movie about the mystical character of Robin Hood.

MAYBE you need as much help as Little John.
If so, get it.

— W. H.

"A man who can still the heart of a lion can stir the heart of a woman."

—From the movie
Samson and Delilah
directed by
Cecil B. DeMille

*"I was known as the bad boy hero of the Marine Corps.
But I've never regretted earning that distinction
because
those were times that demanded
bad boys;
men willing to assert their individuality,
to take risks,
bend rules.
And,
in that regard,
times have not really changed."*

— GREGORY "PAPPY" BOYINGTON
Col., US Marines
Medal of Honor
28 Shoot Downs

*"**We're all in this alone.**"*

—Lily Tomlin

BAD BOYS

—————————————————————————

It has long been understood that you will get very little understanding from other people if you wish to be great in the arts.

You will suffer much abuse. Even those betting on you will doubt you, and there will be times that you must simply shut your ears and endure.

Before you reach a point where you are rewarded adequately or perhaps, extravagantly, for your work…you will be called many things. Among them are:

1. Selfish. (If you really cared for your family you would get a job at McDonald's.)

2. Self-centered. (Who do you think you are, anyway? There are more people in the world besides yourself.)

3. Eccentric. (A misfit…someone who just can't adapt himself to humanity.)

4. And, of course, almost everyone will assume you are gay.

Then, when it all pays off, all will reverse. But what people say will be just as dangerous to your self-esteem. All of a sudden, even your friends (who know you well) will call you by some of the following terms:

1. Genius. (You saw what others didn't, and did it.)

2. Visionary. (You did not let anyone pour water on your fire.)

3. In possession of an iron will. (You did not let anyone stop you.)

4. And, of course, they will still assume you are gay.

Before you get there you will be dragged down far lower than you deserve; after you get there you will be elevated far higher than you deserve. So, you might as well do it your own way. And, if you are going to do it your own way,
             you might as well
                be bad.

—W. H.

*"IF the world won't speak my name
with awe and deference,
at least I will;
and though you may suspect
I am being funny,
I dare you to laugh at me."*

— WHISTLER

Asked why he was so unpleasant to so many people,
he gave this characteristic reply:

*"EARLY in life I made the discovery that I was charming,
and if one is delightful, one has to thrust the world away
to keep from being bored to death."*

— Whistler
The Gentle Art of Making Enemies

"HE took to making a ritual of Sunday breakfasts in his studio for ten
to twenty guests— royalty, social lions, patrons, painters, poets, and journalists.
People were invited for noon, although they might be kept waiting two hours,
with Whistler nowhere to be seen, only heard splashing in his bathtub.
But when he appeared, natty in his white duck suit, fizzing with high spirits
and funny stories, everybody forgave him."

— *The World of Whistler*
Tom Prideaux
and editors of Time/Life Books

Boston, Charles, xethro Tull,
Los Lobos

*"**LEADERSHIP** is primarily a high-powered, right brain activity. It's more of an art..."*

—STEVEN R. COVEY
The Seven Habits of Highly Effective People

ON LEADERSHIP

I write this letter for several reasons:
1. I want you to get the straight stuff. There is just too much extraneous garbage going around. I'd like to see you get into the vein, where the blood is.

2. To give me a way of tackling all the necessary issues in life one by one. It all appears too complex to the beginning struggler. I hate that. I think it is my obligation to help you keep it simple.

3. To motivate myself by forcing myself to narrow down to the real tasks at hand. A keen eye is a means of survival. I want to keep one... and help you, too.

Now for leadership... what is it?

I have made it one of my life's tasks to know what leadership is all about. I have read books by the score with that intent alone ... and I have watched. I have watched people do it... and not do it... and I'll keep on watching.

To condense it all, I would say that a leader embodies the following three ideals:

IDEAL NUMBER ONE: He is what he wants others to be.

The greatest power on earth is example. Imitation is the greatest and quickest way to learn. Just *show* me. The greatest learning experience I ever had in drawing was not drawing on my own, but watching my mother draw. There is just something phenomenal about *watching someone go where you want to go*. I have read about this happening in so many lives like **Hannibal, Patton, Puller, Rubens, J. Hudson Taylor, Dawson Trotman, Jim Elliot.**

IDEAL NUMBER TWO: He is able to boil off the fat, and put the picture on the wall.

Men don't just need example, but also vision. That was **Turner's** weakness. He couldn't put his ideas into words in order to help feed the fire of the younger ones. He was a master of painting... an "unbelievable" example... but a failure at communication. He could show people how, but he couldn't tell them why.

That's what I appreciate about **Watchman Nee**. He not only embodied what he believed, but had a way of recruiting me to it with his pen. He helped clean out the cobweb... and showed me the game real spiders play.

I have read about that ability in **Tolstoy**. I think, too, about **David Brainerd, Adoniram Judson,** and **Alexander Solzhenitzen.**

IDEAL NUMBER THREE: He cares about people.

This is the real exciting one. Why they care about people is a different issue. For example, one could get all hung up on the reality of megalomania in a person like **MacArthur**. Someone may care about people for the wrong reasons, but the fact remains that he was a good leader.

You see, it is one thing to be an example, and another to speak in such a way as to make it all look very simple to others. However, to care enough about people to actually lead them into a better way is quite another matter altogether.

That's why I respect men who did something in the company of others also committed to the task at hand. **MacArthur**, for example, is to be admired for the great economy of life he practiced in WWII. All his people were committed to by-passing a fight in order to get to the objective. **MacArthur** cared about people. **Nimitz**, on the other hand, slaughtered them.

Consider **Billy Graham**. He was never caught up in all the religious rigmarole that our "American Christians" are famous for. He just cares about people, and helps lead them into a life-style that he both embodies and defends. He has helped me keep the whole love-affair with **Christ** as simple as it should be.

> *"THERE is no such thing as bad regiments, only bad colonels."*
>
> — NAPOLEON

IN summary then, I see three ideals in the great leaders I have become familiar with:

ONE: They are an example of what you want to be in any given context. *They give you someone to imitate* (learn from).

TWO: They help you see the big banana, and how you fit under the peeling. *They give you a vision...the big picture.*

THREE: They care about you enough to challenge you personally into a significant change. They ask you to follow. *They give you something that you can live for* in your own slot in time and space. More importantly, they give you something to die for. They help provide you with a gap to plug.

Want it real simple?
>   They give an *example* (what).
>   They provide a *vision* (why).
>   They give you a *task* (how).

Leaders are gifts... but one gone bad makes quite a stink!

CHOOSE them carefully.

— W. H.

FOLLOWING YOUR EYE

Do you have a good eye?

WOULD you maintain a picture was good even if eight or ten people vehemently disagreed with you?

Do you have the guts to follow your eye?

If you wouldn't dare, I know why.

1. *You have been wrong before.* It is not that you lack conviction, nor diction. It is just that you respect the fact that you know how emotion can cloud vision. Right? How many times have you been caught up in the good part of a painting without being able to see that the "whole" painting didn't work? For the first couple of years of this "full-time" business I *had* to get someone else to help me decide what was good enough to mat. Gut wrenching to do it alone!

2. *There are too many art forms to be good at them all.* For example, while viewing a "World Tour" of prints in the El Paso Museum of Art, I was struck with the insanity of it all. I found it hard to believe what I thought was an incredible lack of taste in the choice of subject matter. "Stupid!" I said. But shortly after I spoke with an informed friend who told me enthusiastically how she was "impressed" by the "craftsmanship." She said the "show" represented great "skill" in the technical aspects of printmaking. While I still thought the show to be an insult, I backed off with vigor in terms of my saying so.

3. *Intimidation.* I remember once watching an actor speak for 30 straight minutes as he portrayed the person of Hitler. I knew he was acting! But so help me, if it was *Hitler*, I would have believed him! Spellbound! I live in fear that *that* actor or his twin would be on the other side of the argument with regard to the merits of a painting I was attempting to defend!

Nevertheless, if you believe it is good, say so. The risks of being wrong, or of being uninformed, or of being intimidated are great. But the hazard of living with the consequences of a lifetime of silence is greater.

Ask for a good eye.

—W. H.

ON SAYING NO

Why is it that to do something free means to others that it is cheap?

Is it weakness on the part of people, when asked to volunteer, to say no? I suggest you be quite careful in this vein. Before volunteering to do anything, make sure to yourself that you were born for the task. Unless the gratitude you receive comes from pleasing God, your good-natured circuits may just short out. People often believe that you said yes to the job because you are bored;

or because you have a compulsive need to be wanted;

or because you are worthless for tasks of higher claims;

or because you are not good enough at it to be paid for it.

To be candid, stay out of such things, regardless of what people say to convince you otherwise. Unless there is music in your heart at the thought of dancing in this new venture, whether anybody ever sees or notices you, then don't do it.

Say no.

People still think it's cheap if it's free.
And besides, **it is your job to teach the world to paint.**
Are you not *saddened at the sight* of all the mediocre slop called painting that you have seen lately?

— W. H.

"In November of 1880 Whistler returned to London,
    entering, unannounced, the Fine Art Society Exhibition,
    with an extra long cane in one hand
    and the other leading on a leash a white Pomeranian dog.
    'As I walked in,' he recalled later, 'I spoke to no one,
    and putting up my glass I looked at the prints on the wall.'
    'Dear me, dear me!' I said, 'still the same old sad work! Dear me!'"

— *The World of Whistler*
    by Tom Prideaux
    and editors of Time/Life Books

"I have no love for reasonable painting.
The first merit of a picture is to be a feast for the eye."

— EUGENE DELACROIX

THE WONDER OF COLOR

Wow! Every time I look at my raw palette I understand.
Understand what?
The wonder of color.

PEOPLE have argued over it for centuries. Want to hear some of the rhetoric?
Ingres hated it: "Enough of blazing color, it is anti-historical!"

This man was caught up in the thinking of his time: that the highest form of art was historical statement...and all else was second class (like portraits, figures, still life, landscapes, etc.). Telling a story was *it*! He was saying that this idea of "open color" was definitely at odds with the "high calling" of the artist.

Open color consists of two major elements:

     1. The taking of color outside the boundaries of line and form.

     2. The use of color different than that found in the actual motif.

To further understand the statement of Ingres, consider the thinking of *Constable:* "The great vice of the present day is bravura, an attempt to *do something beyond the truth*." In other words...he believed in a concept that did not allow for deviance from the "true" color of something...or someone. Reality was paramount. No distortion. No alteration.

"Open color" was out!

Ah— but there were many who would throw contempt at this target. Like *Gauguin:* "It matters little whether the haystack is yellow or purple, we shall paint it red if we wish." He could indeed care less about historical statement, and felt that there was another calling on *the same level* of historical statement: decoration. In the words of Maurice Denis, "a painting should decorate."

So we see them arguing from two different camps: the commercial establishment saying that truth, reality, and a message were important...and the fine art establishment saying that imagination, distortion and beauty were important. One group detested "blazing color," the other loved it.

Why did they "love it"?

Hear the thoughts of *Delacroix* on the matter: "Color has a much more mysterious and perhaps more powerful force. It acts, so to speak, in spite of us."

Charles Beaudelaire explained: "It seems as if this color thinks by itself independently of the subjects which it clothes."

IN other words, the fine art discipline does not require of an artist the task of evoking a particular mood for the purpose of communicating a message. He is free, then, to use color for the sake of decoration…or beauty…and *let it speak for itself.* Nothing to tell. Nothing to sell. Just art for art's sake. In light of this thinking, Van Gogh said: "I use color in a more *arbitrary manner* to express myself strongly."

If you are "*arbitrary*" in the use of color, as he was, you might also say that you use color:

1. anyway you choose
2. at your discretion
3. unpredictably
4. randomly
5. suddenly
6. impulsively
7. on a whim
8. as a gambler
9. in a fanciful notion
10. extravagantly
11. in a free form
12. betting on an uncertain outcome
13. having an element of risk
14. in a wave of excitement
15. for the fun of it all.

OH! The *wonder* of color.
It speaks.
I flutter.

— W. H.

"*COLOR*
was
not
meant
to
describe,
but
to
arouse
and
excite."

—J. M. W. TURNER

"THE painter is not greatly concerned with objective truth
and the presentation of facts;
what he gives us is his feeling about the facts,
and to do this he conditions color and form as his feeling dictates,
thus he is not a classic but rather an expressionistic painter."

— FREDERIC TAUBES
speaking of Mathias Grünewald
Anatomy of Genius

QUESTION:

Who was Franz Marc?

He was born in the year 1880.
He was killed at Verdun at thirty-six.
One biographer said this about him,

"He used broad planes of brilliant, joyous color bearing no relation to the subject's natural hues... he is famous for his BLUE and RED horses."

—*The Random House Library of Painting and Sculpture*
©Mitchel Beazley Publishers, 1981

QUESTION:

Have you been wailing?

"THIS process of forgetting unimportant details is known as 'abstraction.' Without abstraction, thought is impossible. Some mis-educated people continually interrupt sensible discussion by *wailing*, 'But you have not defined exactly what you mean by this word.' The great majority of words cannot be defined exactly (for instance, the word *RED*). The important thing is not exact definition; it is to know what you are talking about."

— W. W. SAWYER
Assistant Lecturer in Mathematics
Manchester University
Mathematician's Delight, 1946

MODEL IN WATER...

THREE KEYS
TO A SIMPLER LIFE

As I have crossed over the barrier of forty-five years, I find my life loaded, ever more increasingly, with responsibilities. Never have I felt more weight. How can I remain carefree and still find, as well, plenty of simplicity?

I have found these three things of great help:

1. Take time to exercise: I have learned often and well that fresh outlooks make things appear more simple. There is just something about breathing fresh air, looking at the sky, and running that cleans out the brain.

2. Take time to fly: I have learned that God did not give me wings for a reason: He wanted to make airplanes, into which I could be seated, so He could have my full attention. It is out of a jet window that a person is able to look at life in an inverted manner (above the clouds, not below them) and also in a big, expansive way. For example, I am not sure I would have ever *seen* my market until I opened my eyes over Phoenix one day. It made it all so simple after that. It is just a matter of walls …millions of them …and I only need very few to meet my financial goals.

3. Take time to eat chili: I have learned that chili is vital to simplifying a life. First, chili just helps to clean you out so there is less to deal with. Second, research has proven, within only seven shadows of a doubt, that depression is linked to "low chili serum" in the blood. (Depression does not usually happen if a life is too simple.) Besides, I heard that endorphins are released by chili just as much as by exercise. So if you also have natural lithium in your water…you ought to have life by the tail.

> THEREFORE, to keep your life simple,
>   exercise enough,
>   fly enough,
>   and eat enough chili.
>
>   —W. H.

THE DYING MARINE

I met him at a conference years ago: silver hair, a keen sparkle in the eye; funny as all get out, but serious.

Leroy Eims.

He was a Marine who had landed on Iwo Jima. One of his buddies was hit.

It was bad.

He was dying.

Leroy looked him in the eye as his friend desperately asked him what he had to do to get to heaven. Leroy had no answers. His friend died in his arms.

Leroy Eims dedicated his life, then and there, to finding an answer to that question.

Meanwhile, over the years, as he spent his life helping others relate to the One who created them, he saw a lot of people "come and go." Many people confided in him, and told him why they were unhappy *at the end* of their lives.

I was there on campus one day when he decided to tell some of us what he had noticed.

Three common errors.

Three show stoppers.

Three classic ways to ruin your life:

1. "Dabble"....In terms of art a "dabbler" has tried everything. Stitching. Sewing. Painting. Pastel. Watercolor. Water media. Oil. Alkyds. Seminars. Sessions. Workshops.

But they never settle down and *do any one thing well.* They get to the end, and look back on a lifestyle of piddling, fiddling, and dilly-dallying around. They ruin their lives by "dabbling".

2. "Give yourself to a goal...lock, stock and barrel...then get to the end of your life and find out it was the wrong goal." This is a good one. Solomon said, "*Many* plans are in a man's mind, *but* it is the Lord's purpose for him that will stand."

Do you have confidence that the "plan" you have is, in fact, the right one? Are you selling yourself out to something, or someone, that may be, in the end, the wrong goal? Remember, when you get to the end, it is too late to go back on the field. The whistle will have blown. It will be over.

And "over" means "over." *One day you will stand face to face with the unchangeable consequences of your one life.* It will be *too late.* Better look at your options now.

Don't give yourself to the *wrong* goal.

3. "Give in to that lazy, slothful nature and do nothing."

Do *nothing*!

That's a great way to ruin your life…maybe even a classic! You don't even dabble. You just end up never doing anything.

Laziness!

A sloth.

Perhaps you have heard of the "sloth." In nature there are *two kinds*: the three-toed sloth, and the two-toed sloth.

Both are extremely slow-moving mammals.

They both live upside down.

Both let green plants grow on their hair.

Both blend in well with their surroundings.

And so will you, if you do not step out and

Do something!

And that's what he said.

THE silver-haired gentleman had seen *many* well-intentioned people *ruin their lives* because they:

1. Never broke the habit of dabbling.

2. Gave their lives whole-heartedly to the wrong thing.

3. Never, ever really gave themselves to anything at all.

IT is my hope that you do not ruin your life.
You have only *one*.

— W. H.

" TALENT…
something everyone has at twenty-five.
The difficulty is
to have it at fifty."

— EDGAR DEGAS

By the way, what would YOU have told the dying marine?

CHRISTMAS,
TWO DAYS AWAY

*A home full of kids, many memories,
and a realization that many paintings wait to be done.*

COULD any subject intrigue me like the Mother and Child? What was the relationship like between Mary and her son? To have been a miracle, to have conceived, and be a virgin… how could it really be?

To look with a mother's eyes into the child who was, in fact, eternal deity in human flesh…who came mysteriously into her womb—it must have been a thing of rare beauty to behold.

How did she hold him?

How much did she understand?

Did she sing to him?

And watching Him die at the crest of that hill 33 years later…did her songs change?

How many ways did that little baby change her life? Just think, someday we will all have a chance to see the videos…and talk to Mary…and see Jesus.

WE will not meet the baby— but the King.
Are you ready?

— W. H.

❖

"PAINTING is the way to learn to know the maker of all marvelous things— and this is the way to love so great an inventor. For in truth great love springs from the full knowledge of the thing that one loves; and if you do not know it you can love it but little or not at all."

"AND if you love Him for the sake of the good benefits that you expect to obtain from Him, you are like the dog wagging its tail, welcoming and jumping up at the man who may give him a bone. But if the dog knew and would be capable of understanding the virtue of this man how much greater would be his love!"

— LEONARDO DA VINCI
The Artist's Life

"**M**ASTER *those books you have.*
Read them thoroughly.
Bathe in them until they saturate you.
Read and reread them.
Let them go into your very self."

— CHARLES H. SPURGEON

RELEASE ME
& GIVE ME
A BREAK

I am a thief.
I rob and steal ideas and images.
The ideas all come from someone else.
The images all come from someone else.

All of you who want to sue me: prove that what I have done
is not better than what I took.

And, while you are at it, tell me where you got
the ideas and the images I took from you.
Should not Nature sue you if you sue me?

Release me and give me a break.

AND if you don't,
and if you say I am a thief, which I am,
then just know this:

The controversy you stir up
will all be used to write another book,
and I will prosper even more.

So upon second thought, forget what I said and sue me.
My delight will make you squirm,
and my logic will burn your trail.

But if you do it,
do it with class.

"THERE is no merit in
competing with donkeys."
— MARTIAL
circa 40 A. D.

—W. H.

SOMETHING
to help
you
get
ready
to
put
this
book
on
the
shelf:

A friend was trying to knock the gallon can off of Anthony Robert's head as part of an initiation into a rafting and outdoor group called "Mountain Men Anonymous." His friend used a bow and arrow, and, of course, missed. The arrow tip went ten inches into his brain. Although he lost his right eye, he survived the accident. But his survival was possible only after the surgeons drilled a larger hole around the tip of the arrow at the back of his head and pulled it out.

— *El Paso Times*, May 6, 1993

"I don't think that's a good initiation.
I think a hug would be better."

— ANTHONY ROBERTS, Age 25

"A
*great book
should leave you
with many experiences
and
slightly exhausted
at the end."*

— WILLIAM STYRON
Quoted by Malcolm Cowley
in *Writers at Work*

YOUNG HORSE @
LOS COLINAS ...

ABOUT THE AUTHOR

WILLIAM ARTHUR HERRING KA, PSA
American Expressionist

BORN with a wild bent for maddening excursions into a world he has little respect for, William Arthur Herring has emerged as a colorful threat to established traditions. A genuine Texas Maverick, he romps with unintimidated zest into the combat zones of the fad-fed zealots of contemporary modern art. Having no regard for the mop-bucket world of "art for art's sake," the artist is a proponent of "beauty for beauty's sake" without the trappings of social propaganda. According to Herring, "the contemporary art movement since and including Picasso may best be described as abject buffoonery matched in absurdity only by Lyndon Baines Johnson, and other associated junior-grade trailblazers."

Equally irreverent in his attitude toward esthetic rules, Herring neither teaches nor practices the use of a focal point, center of interest, and the contrasting of values. He evokes no mood and paints with absolutely no message in mind. Surprisingly, however, the artist is quite contemporary in his artistic manner. For example, in his emotional and expressive drawing style, he often arranges his subject matter against white paper in a two-dimensional flat design, yet dramatically as did the Japanese print artists that pushed individuals like Lautrec, Gauguin and Degas into whole new visual eras. He uses deliberate distortion, and stresses the importance of the use of line as a dynamic element of beauty. His color selection is open and arbitrary. In terms of taste, he adheres to the Hellenistic standards of beauty: *idealization, refinement, and simplicity.*

He also breaks all these rules at his own discretion.

The son of Janet Herring, a celebrated artist, author, and teacher, William Arthur Herring was nurtured by apprenticeship in the wonderfully outrageous world of an artist's home. He currently lives and works about ten miles from that home near Clint, Texas. An outspoken advocate of family life, Herring is married to his wife, Kay…and together they are raising four daughters.

Certainly no stranger to the pulse beat of the art world, Herring was nominated by the Governor of Texas in 1993 for a Presidential appointment to become the Director of the National Endowment for the Arts. Herring is currently President of one of the most prestigious and oldest of the national art societies : Knickerbocker Artists • USA.

A signature member of the Pastel Society of America, he is also the 1990 winner of the "Pastel Society of America Board of Directors Award" presented annually at the National Arts Club. He has also served as a guest instructor for the Parson's School of Design, also in New York. He has exhibited both with the National Academy of Design and the American Watercolor Society, and his works of art are found in such prestigious collections as those of the Santa Fe Railroad, former President Ronald Reagan, and beer baron Peter Coors. Meanwhile, back on the range, the artist recently completed a three-year private investor-financed sabbatical that sent him to paint on location in several exotic places of the world, including Rome, Mexico City, Taxco, The Ruins of Xochicalco, London, Paris, and Venice. He is currently represented by nine galleries in Arizona, Arkansas, New Mexico, Texas, and Virginia .

Politically, William Arthur Herring camps around his own brand of "conservative philosophical anarchy." A graduate of Texas A&M University in International Relations and South American History, he is an outspoken enemy of illegitimate authority, and believes in the overthrow of almost everything. He regards himself as a radical misfit, and reportedly spends the majority of his creative time asleep. He must be regarded as armed and dangerous.

Approach with caution…